Presented by
STAN LEE

The 'Nam Trade Paperback
Published by Marvel Comics,
a New World Pictures Company.
387 Park Avenue South, New York,
New York 10016

Manufactured in the United States of America

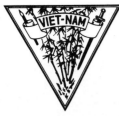

Vietnam. Twenty-five years ago, it was just the name of some insignificant little country in Southeast Asia. Today, it's something much more.

Every American has some opinion on Vietnam and the Vietnamese war. For some, it's the symbol of national disgrace, the war we never should have fought, never should have been involved in. For others, it is a place of memories too terrible to forget.

Ex-grunts (infantrymen), like me, remember it as a place where long periods of boredom were punctuated by eternal moments of terror.

Oddly, though, Vietnam and the war fought there have been generally ignored for the past ten years. Schools devote only a page or so of text to it. Movies and TV shows about it have concentrated on its aftermath and effects on returnees. The actual reality of the war, and its impact on the combatants of both sides, have been largely forgotten.

About a year and a half ago, we decided to create a comic book about Vietnam. We had the best reasons in the world to do it. Time had passed—more than ten years—since the last American chopper lifted off from Saigon. Memories and old antagonisms had been blunted. The country was in a mood for healing, a mood for learning what really happened to that generation of G.I.'s who lived the long conflict in Vietnam.

From this, THE 'NAM was born. The comic was to give a realistic portrayal of the war. The viewpoint is that of the grunts, those ground-pounders who saw the war as a day-to-day struggle for life, who saw in their own superiors an enemy as dreaded as the black-clad "charlie" who materialized out of the darkness of the bush to shoot down a careless troop.

We gave it our best shot, and through the magic of Michael Golden's meticulous artwork and attention to detail, many of you think we've succeeded. THE 'NAM became a success, and we've been telling the story of the men of the 23rd Infantry for almost a year now.

There's a lot of the story yet to tell. We haven't explored Tet yet, or the horror of My Lai. We haven't really shown the problems of the ever-present drugs, or the friction between the races forced into camaraderie in the cauldron of THE 'NAM. But these things are yet to come. In this book, we present the first four issues of the comic series. These are the stories that introduce Ed Marks, Rob Little, Mike Albergo and the rest. The stories that proved to you, the comic reader, that a comic book about the Vietnam War could be a worthwhile investment of your comic-reading money.

So sit back, relax, and enjoy these first four issues. For those of you that haven't read them, I hope they'll give you an idea of what THE 'NAM is all about. For those who have, I hope they'll work as well the second time around.

Adios, and, for my sins, Xin loi,
DOUG MURRAY

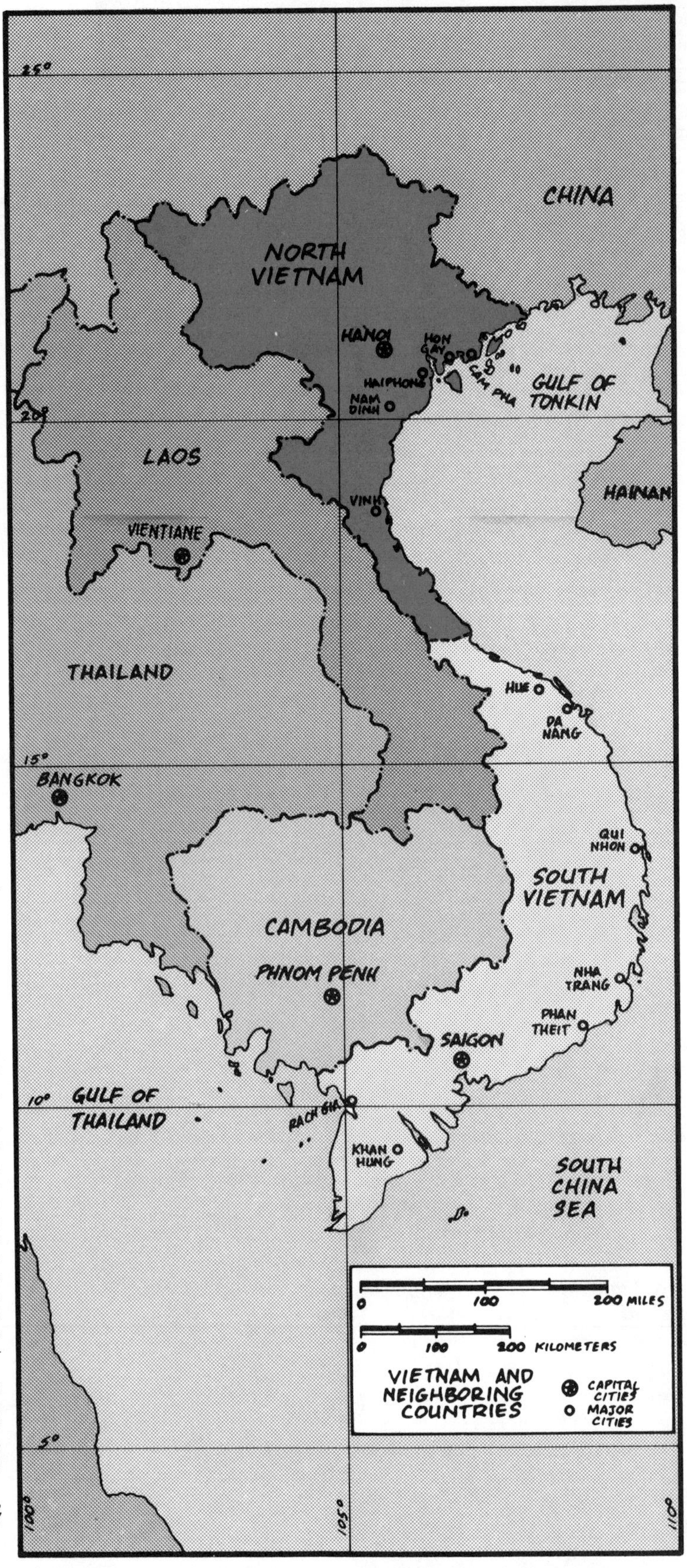

25°
20°
15°
10°
5°
CHINA
NORTH VIETNAM
HANOI
HON GAY
HAIPHONG
CAM PHA
NAM DINH
GULF OF TONKIN
LAOS
HAINAN
VINH
VIENTIANE
THAILAND
HUE
DA NANG
BANGKOK
QUI NHON
SOUTH VIETNAM
CAMBODIA
PHNOM PENH
NHA TRANG
PHAN THEIT
SAIGON
GULF OF THAILAND
RACH GIA
KHAN HUNG
SOUTH CHINA SEA
0 100 200 MILES
0 100 200 KILOMETERS
VIETNAM AND NEIGHBORING COUNTRIES
CAPITAL CITIES
MAJOR CITIES
100°
105°
110°

'NAM NOTES

Private

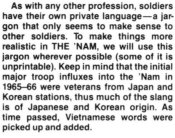

Corporal

Specialist 4

As with any other profession, soldiers have their own private language—a jargon that only seems to make sense to other soldiers. To make things more realistic in THE 'NAM, we will use this jargon wherever possible (some of it is unprintable). Keep in mind that the initial major troop influxes into the 'Nam in 1965–66 were veterans from Japan and Korean stations, thus much of the slang is of Japanese and Korean origin. As time passed, Vietnamese words were picked up and added.

Private First Class

To avoid interfering with the flow of the stories, we have collected the slang terms here, in the glossary, to allow you to check back (or forward) and understand exactly what is being said. We try to be as complete and comprehensive as possible:

AIT: Advanced Individual Training, the Army equivalent of High School. Troops out of basic training get the next level of Army knowledge—usually in their specialty.

APC: Armored Personnel Carrier—specially tooled vehicle armored to keep troops safe from small arms fire (not always too successfully).

AUSSIE: Australian.

BANGALORE: The Bangalore Torpedo was developed during WWII. It was basically a long tube jammed full of explosives. Detonation cord and an electrical detonator are used to set it off. Its shape makes it ideal for pushing under or in front of obstructions, then blowing them out of the way.

11 BUSH: Slang for the Army skill code (11B20) for light weapons infantry. The grunts—the frontline foot soldiers.

COPPED (ONE): Took a hit—got wounded or killed.

DUSTOFF: A helicopter pick-up, usually made in a hurry and under fire. Called this because the chopper raises a bunch of dust, then off it goes.

FAST MOVERS: Fast moving aircraft—jets. Usually used for F-4 Phantoms.

FIRST CAV: The First Air Cavalry—an airborne unit stationed in the 'Nam throughout most of the war.

FLECHETTE: A dart-shaped piece of metal. Hundreds (or thousands) of which were packed into claymores or artillery rounds for the expressed purpose of annihilating closely-packed troops or troops in loose cover.

FIRST SERGEANT: Think of the Army as a big corporation. The officers are the planners, the creators of grand strategies. The grunts are the employees, and the NCO's (Non-Commissioned Officers) are the line managers, the foremen. They're the people who make sure the troops are properly trained, equipped, paid, etc. The First Sergeant, then, is the senior NCO, the man with the most experience and responsibility for the troops. He does most of the administrative work for the company, and is most commonly referred to as simply TOP (for TOP SERGEANT).

GREENIE: A rookie, a new troop, someone without experience.

HAT-UP: Put on your hat and leave. Also SKY-UP and BOOK OUT.

HOOCH: Slang for a hut, house, or barracks. Basically, the place where you live.

KP: Kitchen Police—cleaning up after the troops eat—you know, the work Mom always does at home.

KLICKS: Kilometers—about two-thirds of a mile.

LPC: Leadership Potential Candidate. A short army school, usually following Basic Training for Individuals the Army considers to have shown leadership qualifications. Candidates are given some extra training to speed their development.

LZ: Landing Zone, a cleared area big enough for a helicopter to land (or hover close to the ground) long enough to pick up or put down troops.

Sergeant

Specialist 5

Staff Sergeant

Specialist 6

Sergeant First Class

Master Sergeant

MEDIVAC: An evacuation for medical purposes. Done by specially equipped and manned choppers used to pick up wounded men and keep them alive while rushing them to hospital.

MILK RUN: Leftover term from WWII. A really easy mission, probably referring to how peaceful it is in the early morning when the milkman made his rounds.

MOS KOSHEE: Japanese phrase adopted for use in the 'NAM, generally used to mean 'right now' or 'right away.'

M-16 (14): The basic weapon of the Infantry. The M-14 was chambered for the NATO 7.62mm round and was used until the mid 1960's when it was replaced by the lighter, more versatile, M-16 which fired the smaller, faster 5.56mm round and enabled the grunt to hump more ammo.

NO SWEAT-DE-DA: Phrase of American/Vietnamese origin, commonly used to mean something really easy to do.

PAUL REVERE/THAN PHONG 14: A combined U.S./South Vietnamese operation to pacify large pieces of territory and clean out several VC strong points. Lasted from May of 1966 until the following September.

POP SOME CAPS: Fire your rifle, usually on full automatic. From the childhood use of a cap pistol and the similarity in sound to an M-16 in action.

QUAD 50: A weapon developed in WWII for Air Defense. Four 50 caliber machine guns mounted on a single frame to allow them to shoot at the same point.

R&R: Rest and Recreation.

REPO DEPOT: Replacement Depot. A staging area where new troops and other replacements were housed while their records were checked and updated, medical checks were made, and necessary equipment issued before moving to a frontline unit.

ROCK AND ROLL: Letting it all hang out—using the M-16 in full automatic, as a small sub-machine gun.

ROLLED: Robbed. Probably started because people rolled their victims over onto their backs to get at their wallets.

RVN: The REPUBLIC OF VIET NAM, more specifically, South Viet Nam.

SAPPED: Hit over the head—in this term, usually with a blackjack.

SEATAC: Seattle-Tacoma Airport. Closest internation airport to Ft. Lewis, Washington and connecting point for many troops on their way to the 'Nam.

SHORT: Almost at the end of a tour—short of time (remaining).

SHRAPNEL: Named for an English Artillery Officer. Pieces of metal that come from explosives, shells, or mines. Literally used as any piece of metal, other than a bullet, which caused a wound.

SLICK: Reference to the UH-1. The troop-carrying version of the ubiquitous HUEY Helicopter.

SPEC 5: Specialist Fifth Class. Equivalent to a Buck Sergeant.

TOP: First Sergeant.

UNCLE SUGAR: Uncle Sam—the congress, the fat cats back home.

VICTOR CHARLIE: Sometimes just 'CHARLIE' or 'CHARLES.' The Viet Cong—the enemy.

"THE WORLD": The good ol' USA. Home, the real world to those in the never-never land of the 'NAM.

"YOU CAN TELL IT'S MATTEL": When troops first saw the M-16 which is primarily made of plastic, they jokingly used the phrase Mattel Toys had used as an advertising slogan for their (plastic) toys.

Above:

Typical Claymore mine and detonator

Below: Blast diagram of Claymore with killing and wounding radii

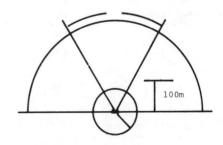

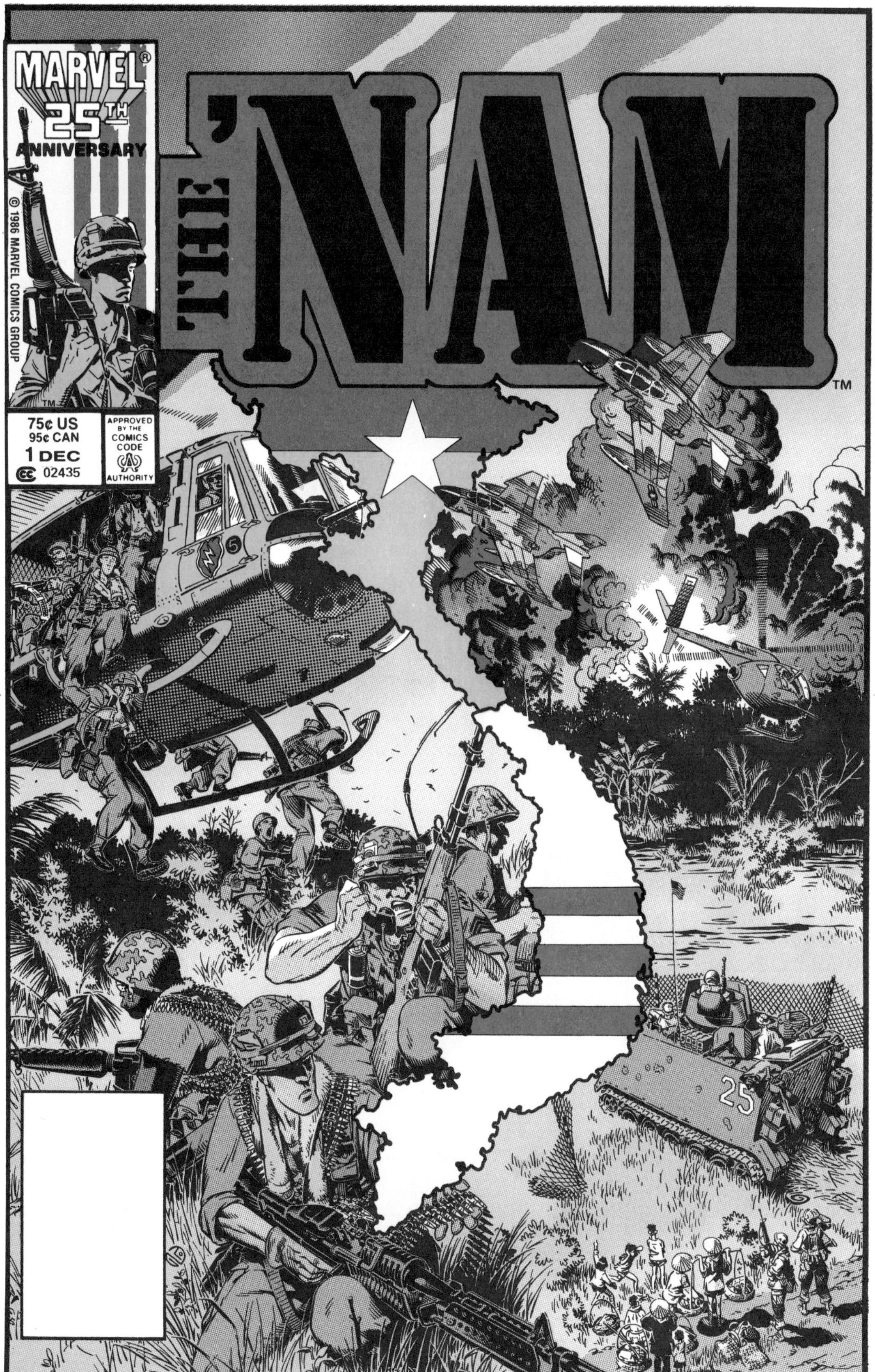
MARVEL®
25TH
ANNIVERSARY
© 1986 MARVEL COMICS GROUP
THE 'NAM
TM
75¢ US
95¢ CAN
1 DEC
02435
APPROVED BY THE COMICS CODE AUTHORITY
25

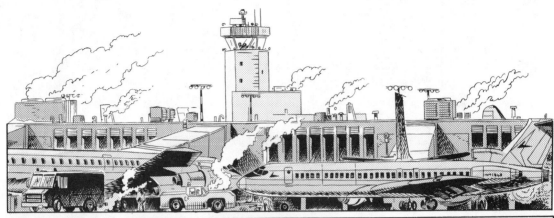

EARLY IN 1966, A YOUNG SOLDIER LEAVES HOME FOR HIS FIRST TASTE OF INDEPENDENCE, AND **WAR**.

'NAM: FIRST PATROL

STORY: DOUG MURRAY. PENCILS, COLORING:
MICHAEL GOLDEN. INKS: ARMANDO GIL.
LETTERS: PHIL FELIX. EDITOR: LARRY HAMA.
EDITOR IN CHIEF: JIM SHOOTER.

GOODBYE, SON! DON'T FORGET TO WRITE! PLEASE... BE CAREFUL!

THAT'S RIGHT, SON! BE CAREFUL!

DON'T FORGET YOUR DRAMAMINE!

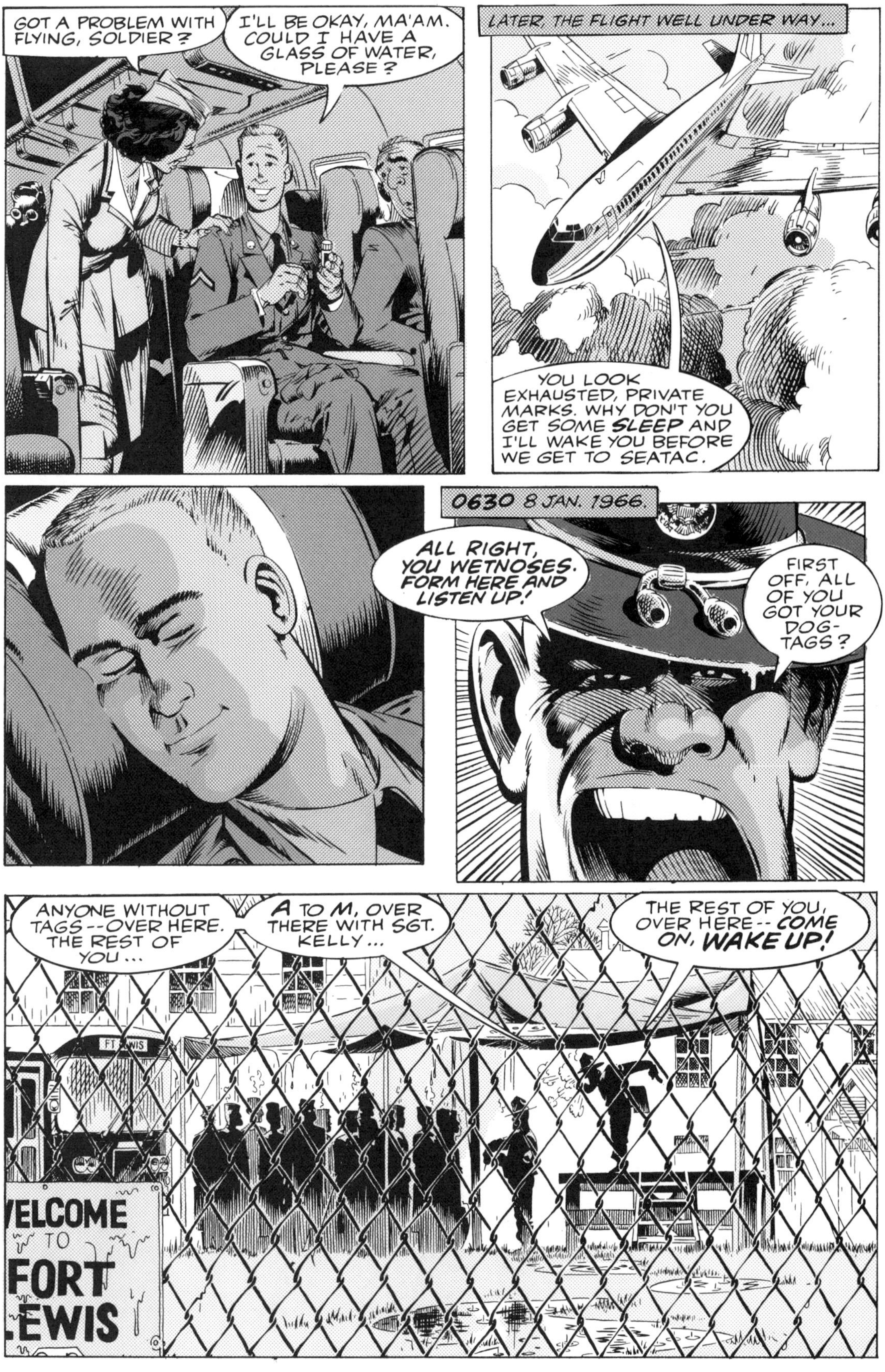
GOT A PROBLEM WITH FLYING, SOLDIER?
I'LL BE OKAY, MA'AM. COULD I HAVE A GLASS OF WATER, PLEASE?
LATER, THE FLIGHT WELL UNDER WAY...
YOU LOOK EXHAUSTED, PRIVATE MARKS. WHY DON'T YOU GET SOME SLEEP AND I'LL WAKE YOU BEFORE WE GET TO SEATAC.
0630 8 JAN. 1966.
ALL RIGHT, YOU WETNOSES. FORM HERE AND LISTEN UP!
FIRST OFF, ALL OF YOU GOT YOUR DOG-TAGS?
ANYONE WITHOUT TAGS--OVER HERE. THE REST OF YOU...
A TO M, OVER THERE WITH SGT. KELLY...
THE REST OF YOU, OVER HERE--COME ON, WAKE UP!
FT LEWIS
VELCOME TO FORT LEWIS

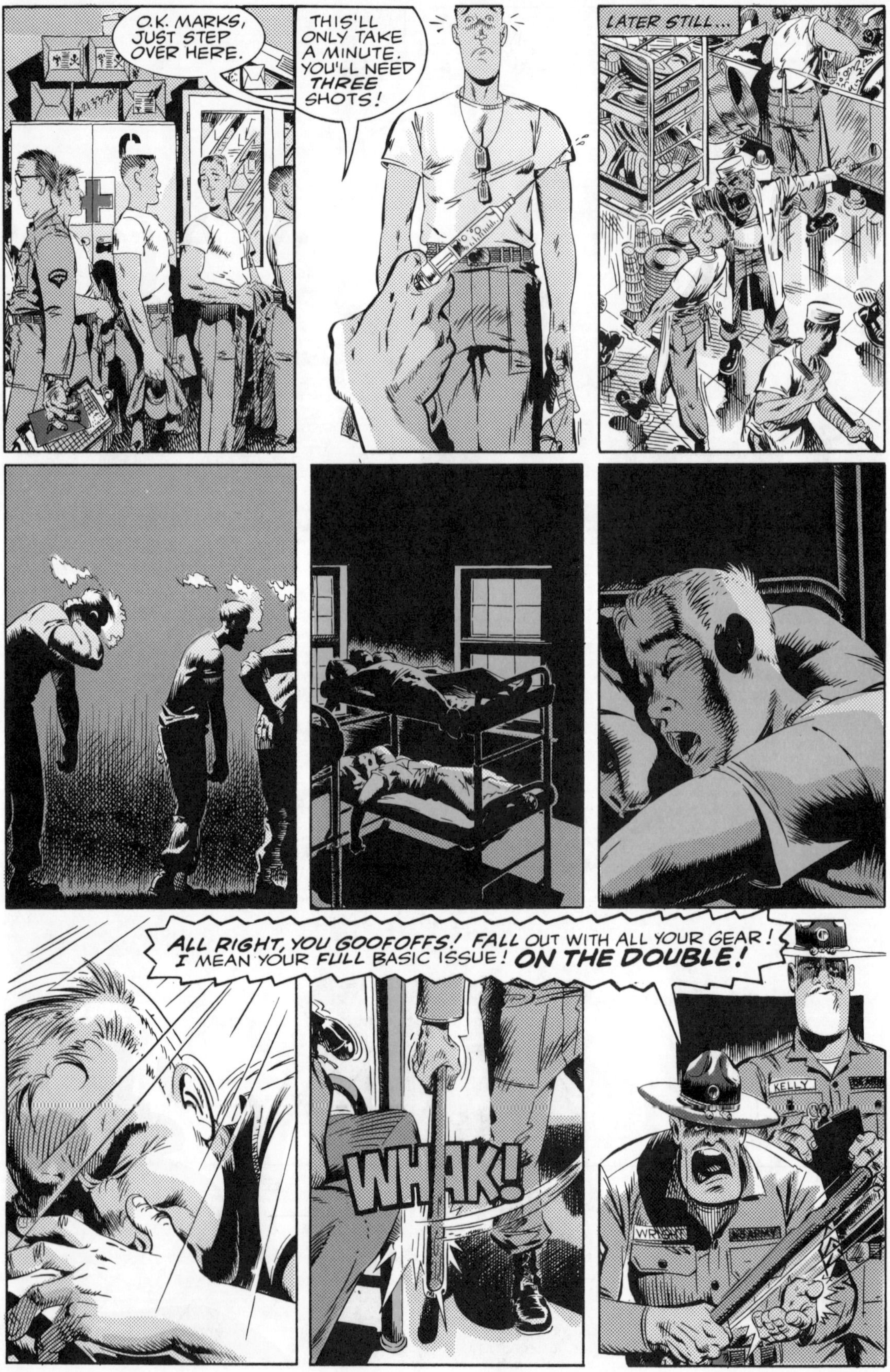
O.K. MARKS, JUST STEP OVER HERE.
THIS'LL ONLY TAKE A MINUTE. YOU'LL NEED THREE SHOTS!
LATER STILL...
ALL RIGHT, YOU GOOFOFFS! FALL OUT WITH ALL YOUR GEAR! I MEAN YOUR FULL BASIC ISSUE! ON THE DOUBLE!
WHAK!
KELLY

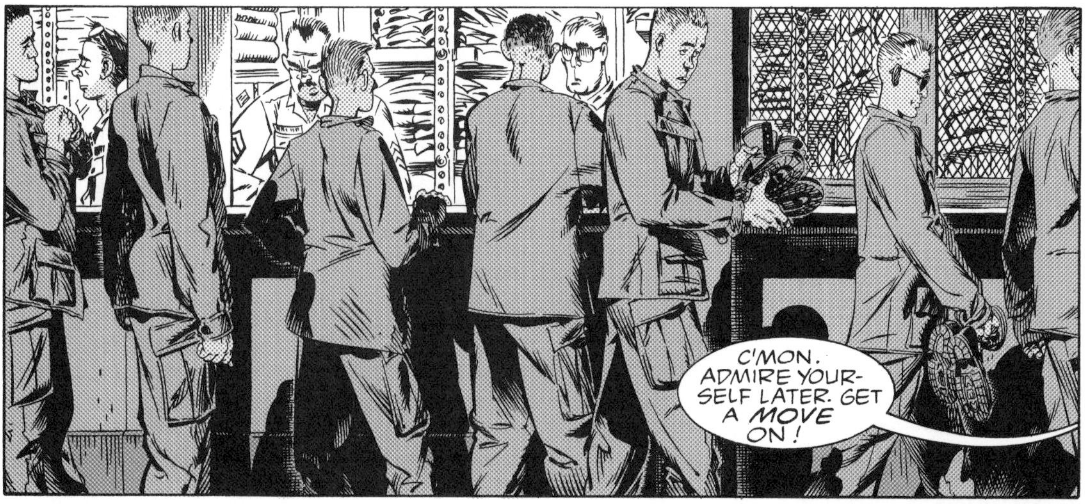
C'MON. ADMIRE YOUR-SELF LATER. GET A MOVE ON!

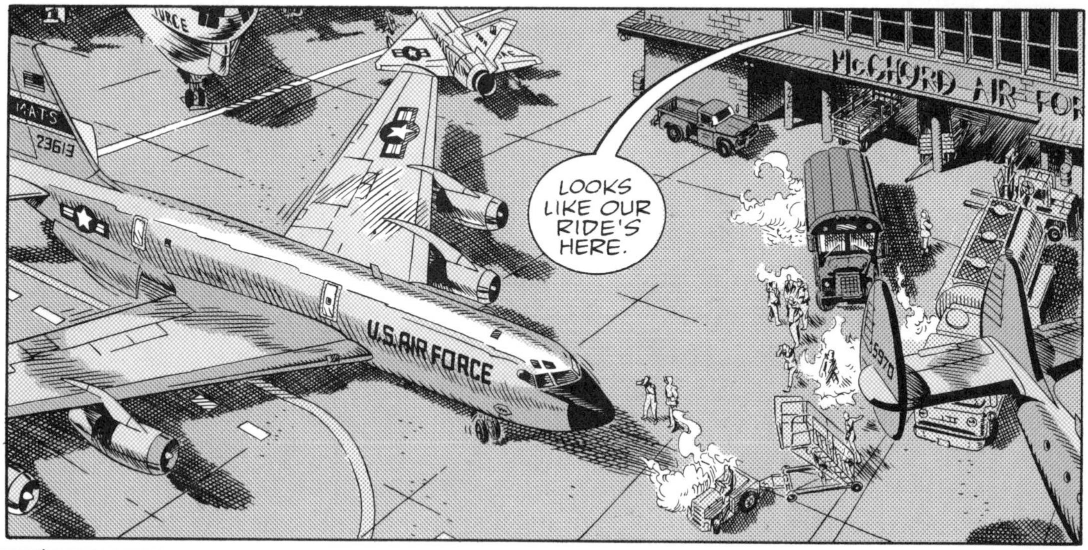
LOOKS LIKE OUR RIDE'S HERE.
U.S. AIR FORCE

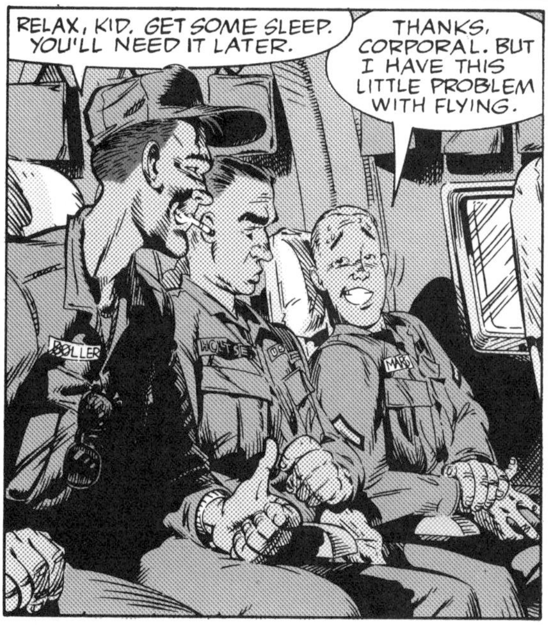
RELAX, KID. GET SOME SLEEP. YOU'LL NEED IT LATER.
THANKS, CORPORAL. BUT I HAVE THIS LITTLE PROBLEM WITH FLYING.

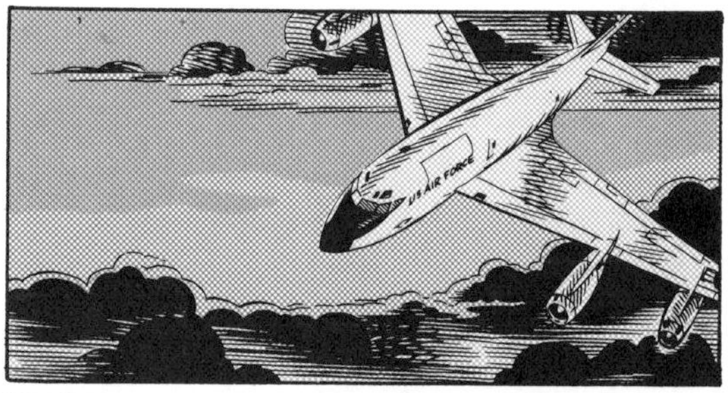

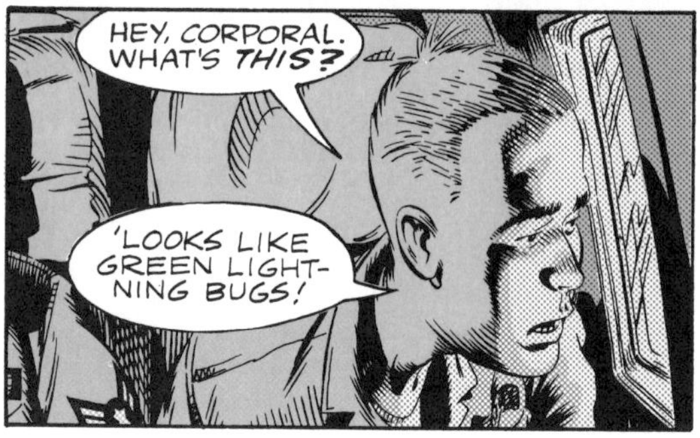
HEY, CORPORAL. WHAT'S THIS?
'LOOKS LIKE GREEN LIGHT-NING BUGS!

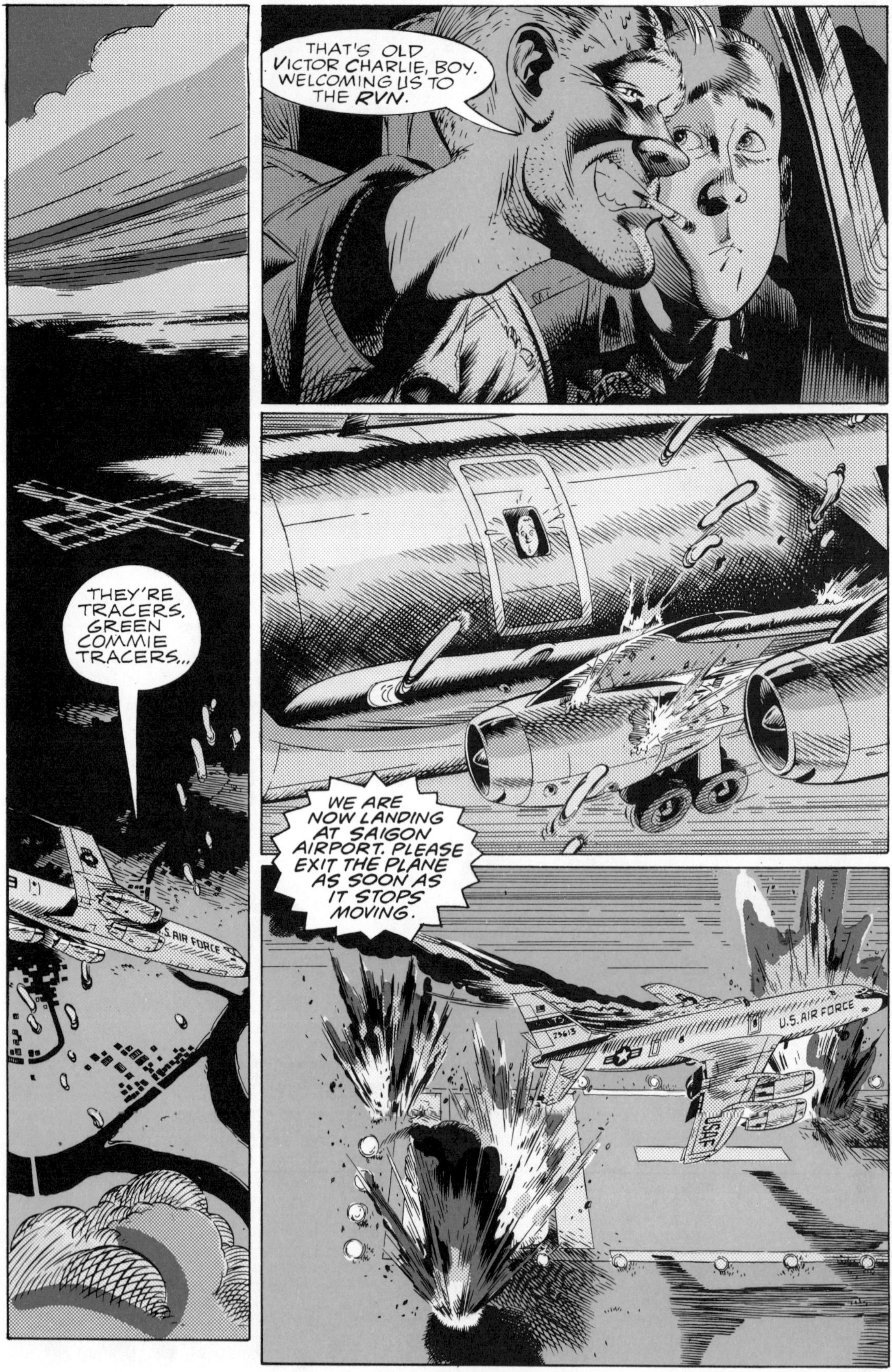
THAT'S OLD VICTOR CHARLIE, BOY. WELCOMING US TO THE RVN.
THEY'RE TRACERS. GREEN COMMIE TRACERS...
U.S. AIR FORCE
WE ARE NOW LANDING AT SAIGON AIRPORT. PLEASE EXIT THE PLANE AS SOON AS IT STOPS MOVING.
U.S. AIR FORCE
USAF

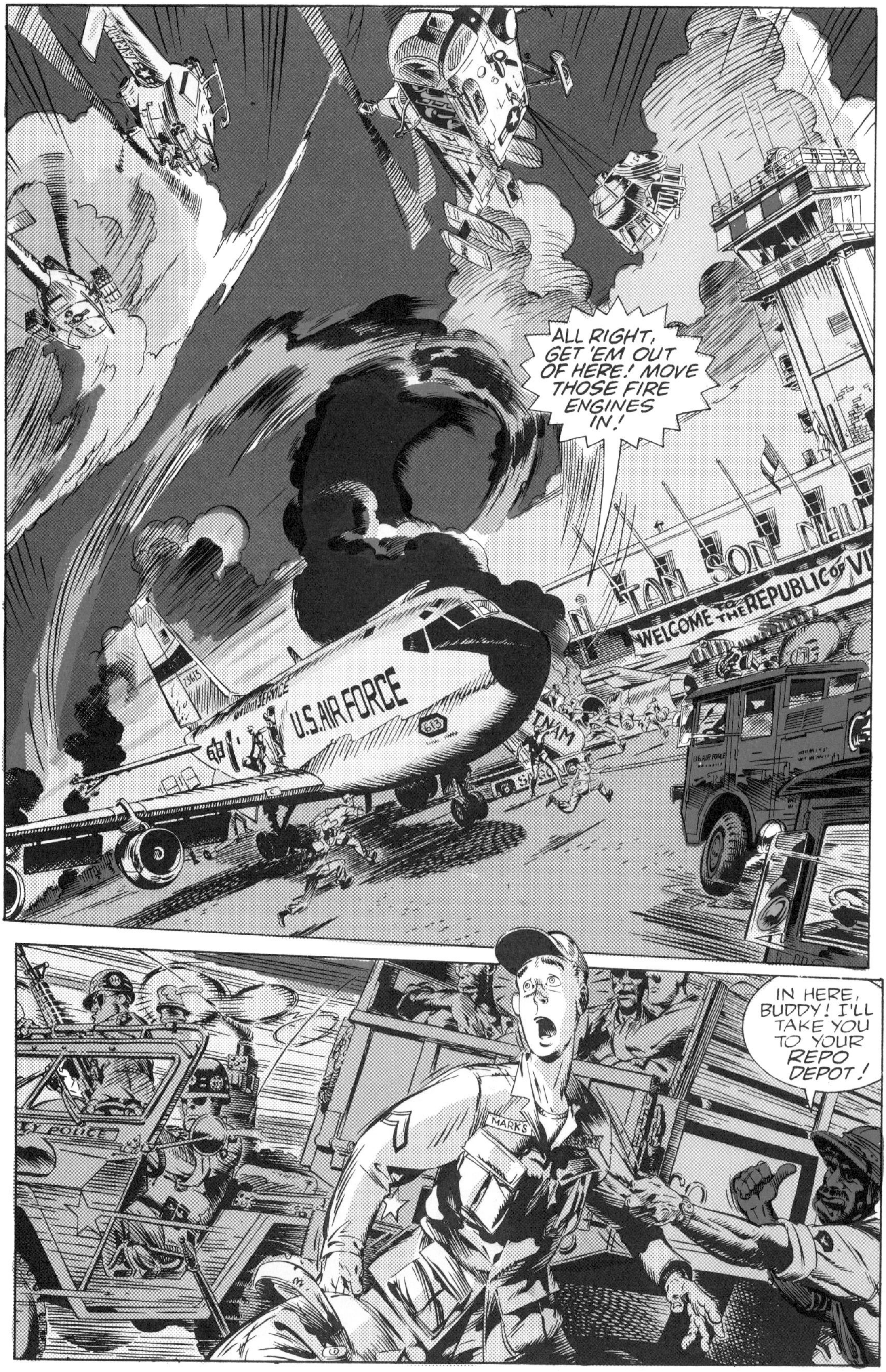
ALL RIGHT, GET 'EM OUT OF HERE! MOVE THOSE FIRE ENGINES IN!
U.S. AIR FORCE
MARKS
IN HERE, BUDDY! I'LL TAKE YOU TO YOUR REPO DEPOT!

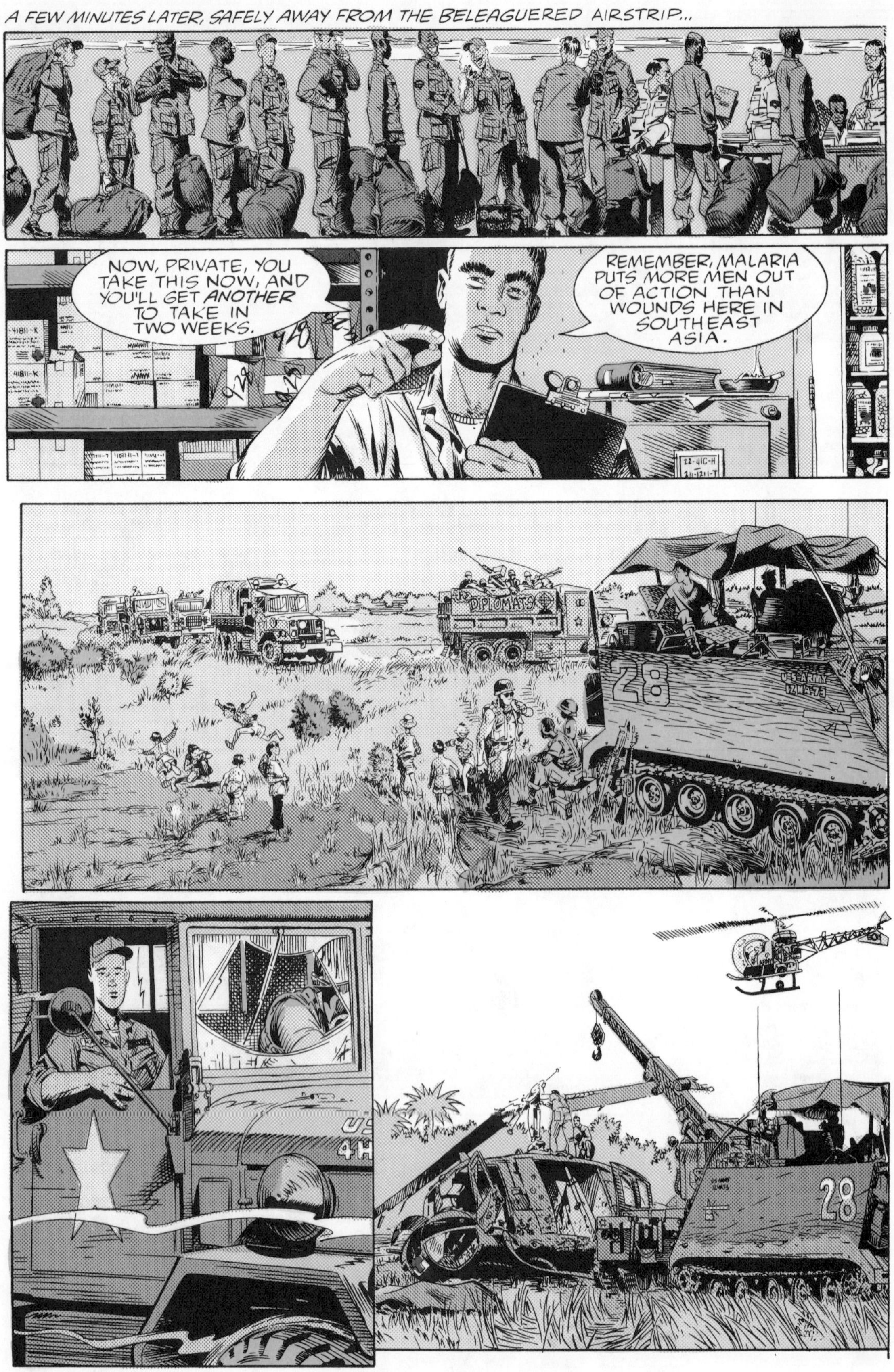
A FEW MINUTES LATER, SAFELY AWAY FROM THE BELEAGUERED AIRSTRIP...
NOW, PRIVATE, YOU TAKE THIS NOW, AND YOU'LL GET ANOTHER TO TAKE IN TWO WEEKS.
REMEMBER, MALARIA PUTS MORE MEN OUT OF ACTION THAN WOUNDS HERE IN SOUTHEAST ASIA.

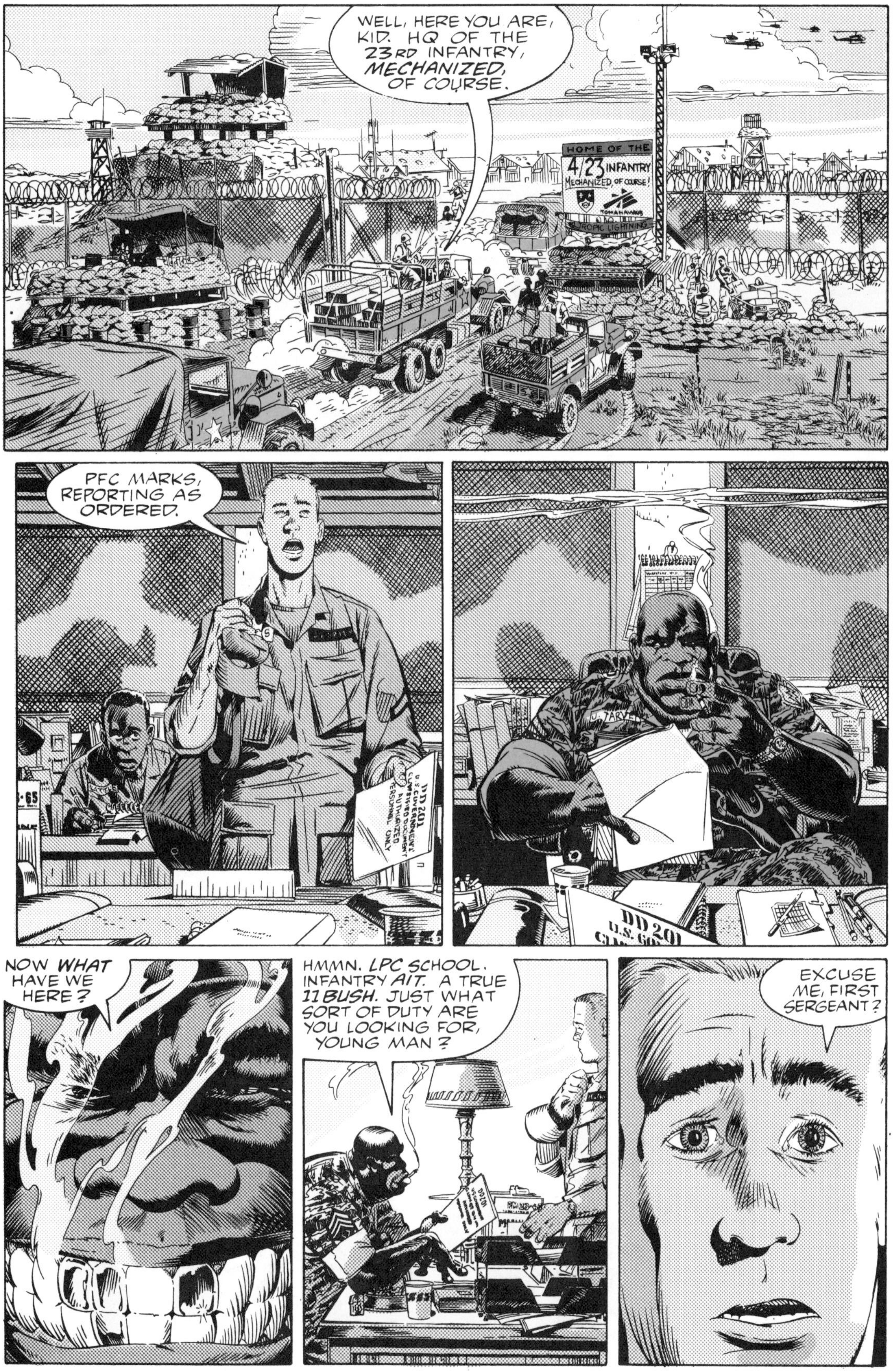
WELL, HERE YOU ARE, KID. HQ OF THE 23RD INFANTRY, MECHANIZED, OF COURSE.
HOME OF THE
4/23 INFANTRY
MECHANIZED, OF COURSE!
PFC MARKS, REPORTING AS ORDERED.
NOW WHAT HAVE WE HERE?
HMMN. LPC SCHOOL. INFANTRY AIT. A TRUE 11 BUSH. JUST WHAT SORT OF DUTY ARE YOU LOOKING FOR, YOUNG MAN?
EXCUSE ME, FIRST SERGEANT?

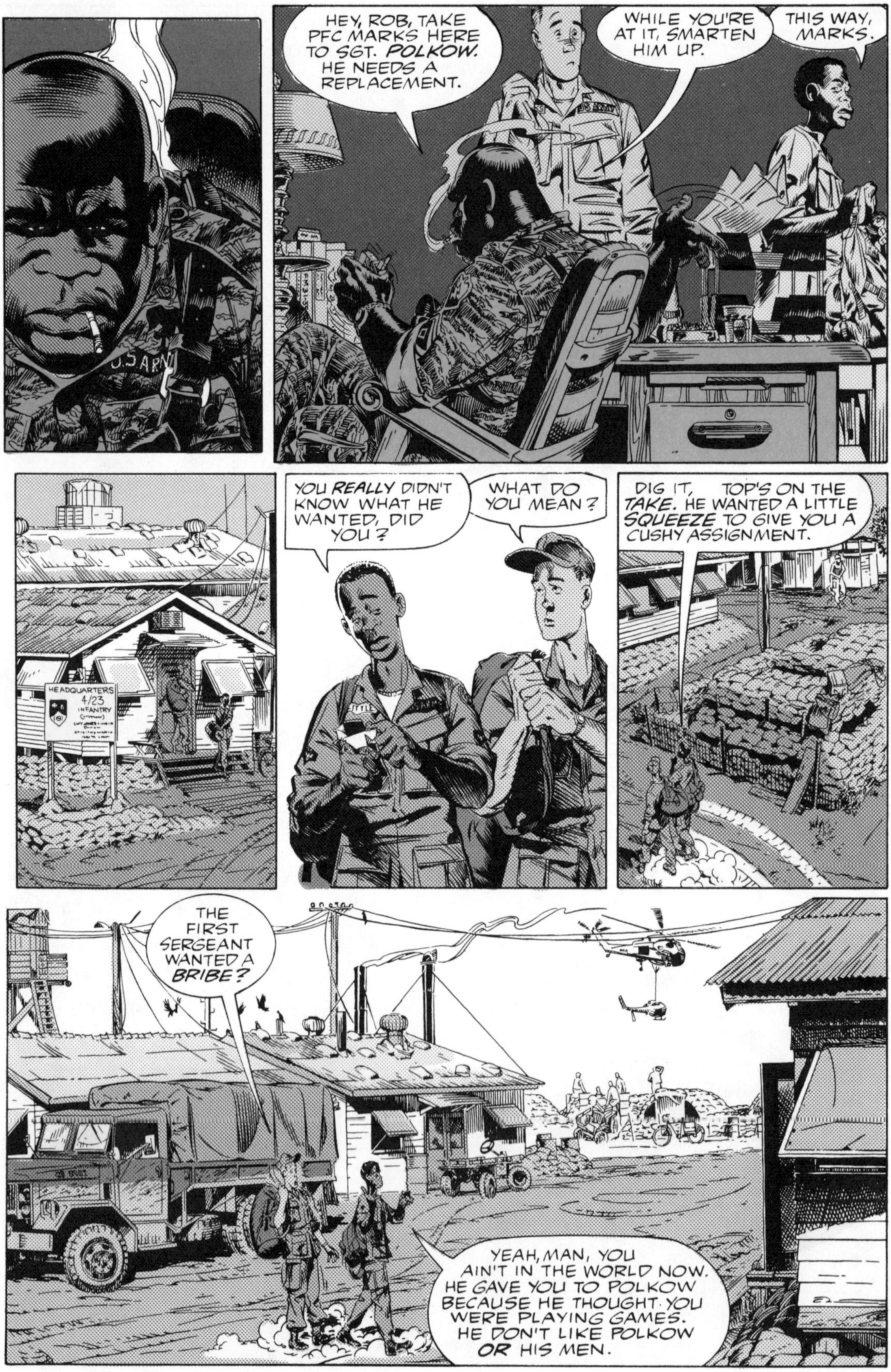
HEY, ROB, TAKE PFC MARKS HERE TO SGT. POLKOW. HE NEEDS A REPLACEMENT.
WHILE YOU'RE AT IT, SMARTEN HIM UP.
THIS WAY, MARKS.
HEADQUARTERS 4/23 INFANTRY
YOU REALLY DIDN'T KNOW WHAT HE WANTED, DID YOU?
WHAT DO YOU MEAN?
DIG IT, TOP'S ON THE TAKE. HE WANTED A LITTLE SQUEEZE TO GIVE YOU A CUSHY ASSIGNMENT.
THE FIRST SERGEANT WANTED A BRIBE?
YEAH, MAN, YOU AIN'T IN THE WORLD NOW. HE GAVE YOU TO POLKOW BECAUSE HE THOUGHT YOU WERE PLAYING GAMES. HE DON'T LIKE POLKOW OR HIS MEN.

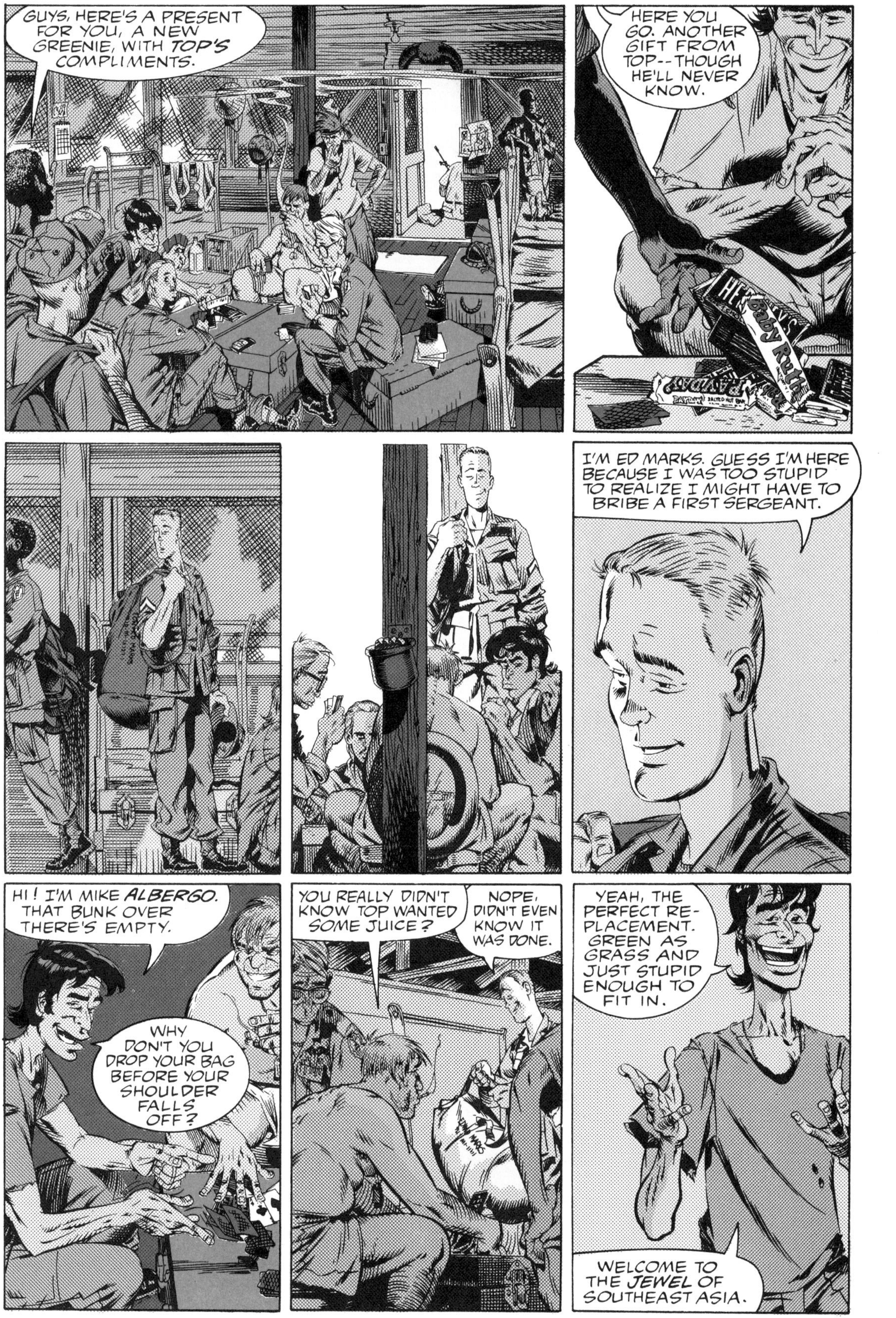
GUYS, HERE'S A PRESENT FOR YOU, A NEW GREENIE, WITH TOP'S COMPLIMENTS.
HERE YOU GO. ANOTHER GIFT FROM TOP--THOUGH HE'LL NEVER KNOW.
I'M ED MARKS. GUESS I'M HERE BECAUSE I WAS TOO STUPID TO REALIZE I MIGHT HAVE TO BRIBE A FIRST SERGEANT.
HI! I'M MIKE ALBERGO. THAT BUNK OVER THERE'S EMPTY.
WHY DON'T YOU DROP YOUR BAG BEFORE YOUR SHOULDER FALLS OFF?
YOU REALLY DIDN'T KNOW TOP WANTED SOME JUICE?
NOPE, DIDN'T EVEN KNOW IT WAS DONE.
YEAH, THE PERFECT RE-PLACEMENT. GREEN AS GRASS AND JUST STUPID ENOUGH TO FIT IN.
WELCOME TO THE JEWEL OF SOUTHEAST ASIA.

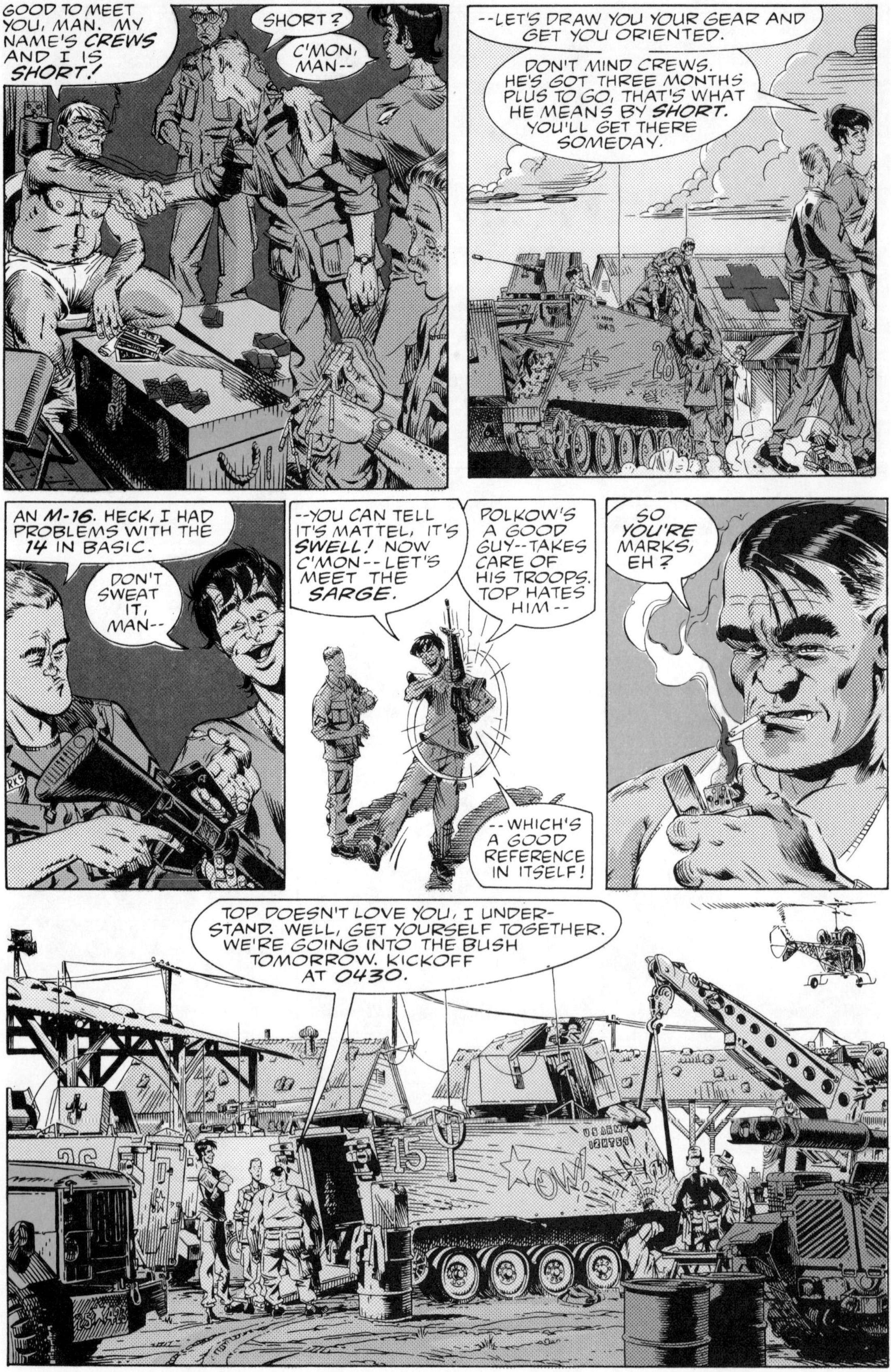
GOOD TO MEET YOU, MAN. MY NAME'S CREWS AND I IS SHORT!
SHORT?
C'MON, MAN--
--LET'S DRAW YOU YOUR GEAR AND GET YOU ORIENTED.
DON'T MIND CREWS. HE'S GOT THREE MONTHS PLUS TO GO, THAT'S WHAT HE MEANS BY SHORT. YOU'LL GET THERE SOMEDAY.
AN M-16. HECK, I HAD PROBLEMS WITH THE 14 IN BASIC.
DON'T SWEAT IT, MAN--
--YOU CAN TELL IT'S MATTEL, IT'S SWELL! NOW C'MON--LET'S MEET THE SARGE.
POLKOW'S A GOOD GUY--TAKES CARE OF HIS TROOPS. TOP HATES HIM--
--WHICH'S A GOOD REFERENCE IN ITSELF!
SO YOU'RE MARKS, EH?
TOP DOESN'T LOVE YOU, I UNDERSTAND. WELL, GET YOURSELF TOGETHER. WE'RE GOING INTO THE BUSH TOMORROW. KICKOFF AT 0430.
OW!

KEEP YOUR EYES OPEN. THIS'S A SEARCH AND DESTROY. IT'S LIKE QUAIL HUNTING, YOU FLUSH 'EM AND SHOOT 'EM AS THEY RISE.

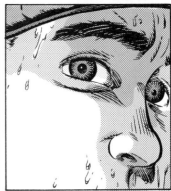

MIKE, GOT A JOB FOR YOU, I THINK!

C'MON ED, STICK WITH ME.

LOOKS LIKE YOU'RE RIGHT, SARGE. BOOBY TRAP.

SEE, CHARLIE BURIES THESE WITH THE PLUNGER UP. SOME POOR JERK STEPS ON IT, AND...

...WHAMO!

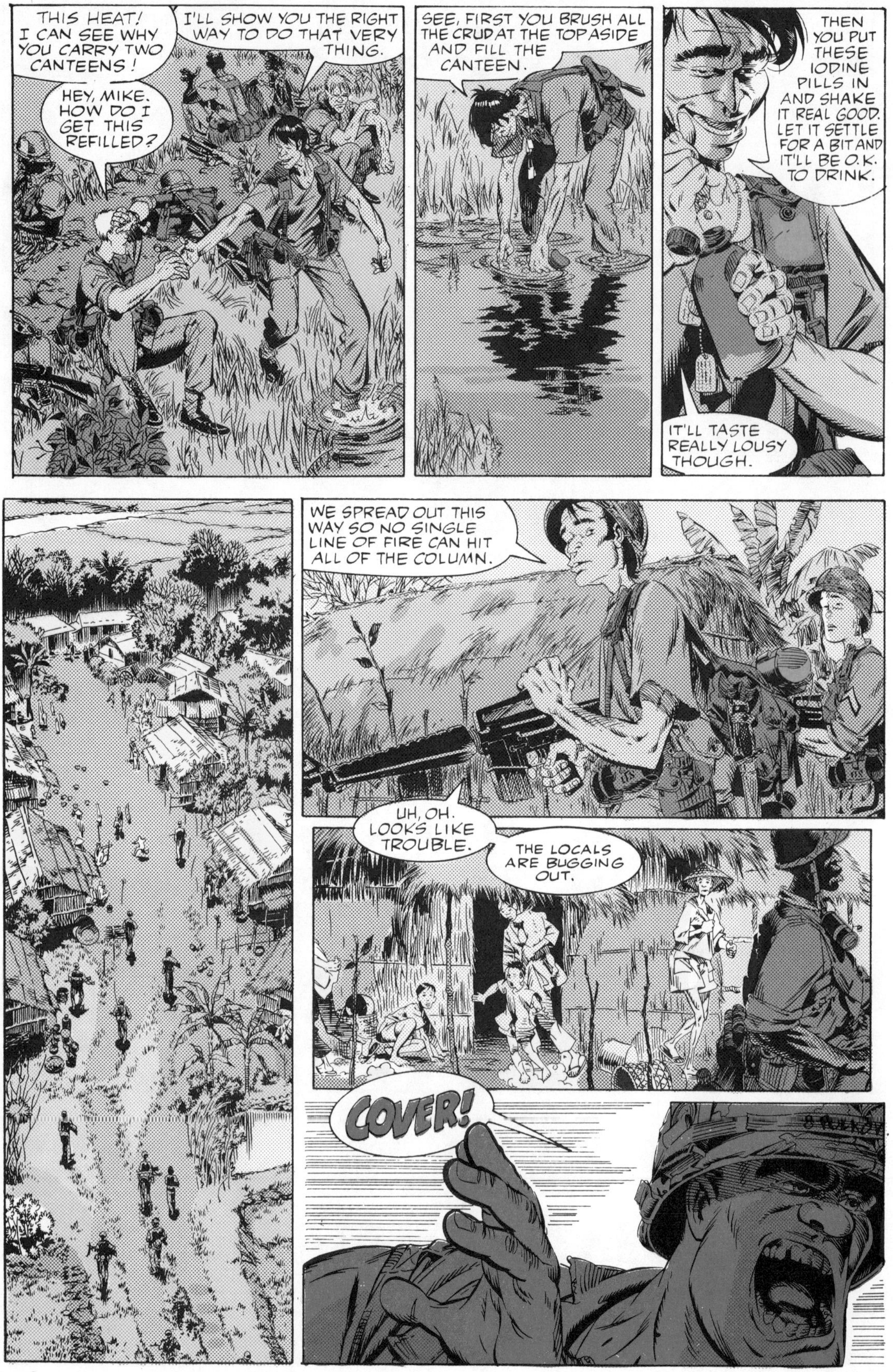
THIS HEAT! I CAN SEE WHY YOU CARRY TWO CANTEENS!
HEY, MIKE. HOW DO I GET THIS REFILLED?
I'LL SHOW YOU THE RIGHT WAY TO DO THAT VERY THING.
SEE, FIRST YOU BRUSH ALL THE CRUD AT THE TOP ASIDE AND FILL THE CANTEEN.
THEN YOU PUT THESE IODINE PILLS IN AND SHAKE IT REAL GOOD. LET IT SETTLE FOR A BIT AND IT'LL BE O.K. TO DRINK.
IT'LL TASTE REALLY LOUSY THOUGH.
WE SPREAD OUT THIS WAY SO NO SINGLE LINE OF FIRE CAN HIT ALL OF THE COLUMN.
UH, OH. LOOKS LIKE TROUBLE.
THE LOCALS ARE BUGGING OUT.
COVER!

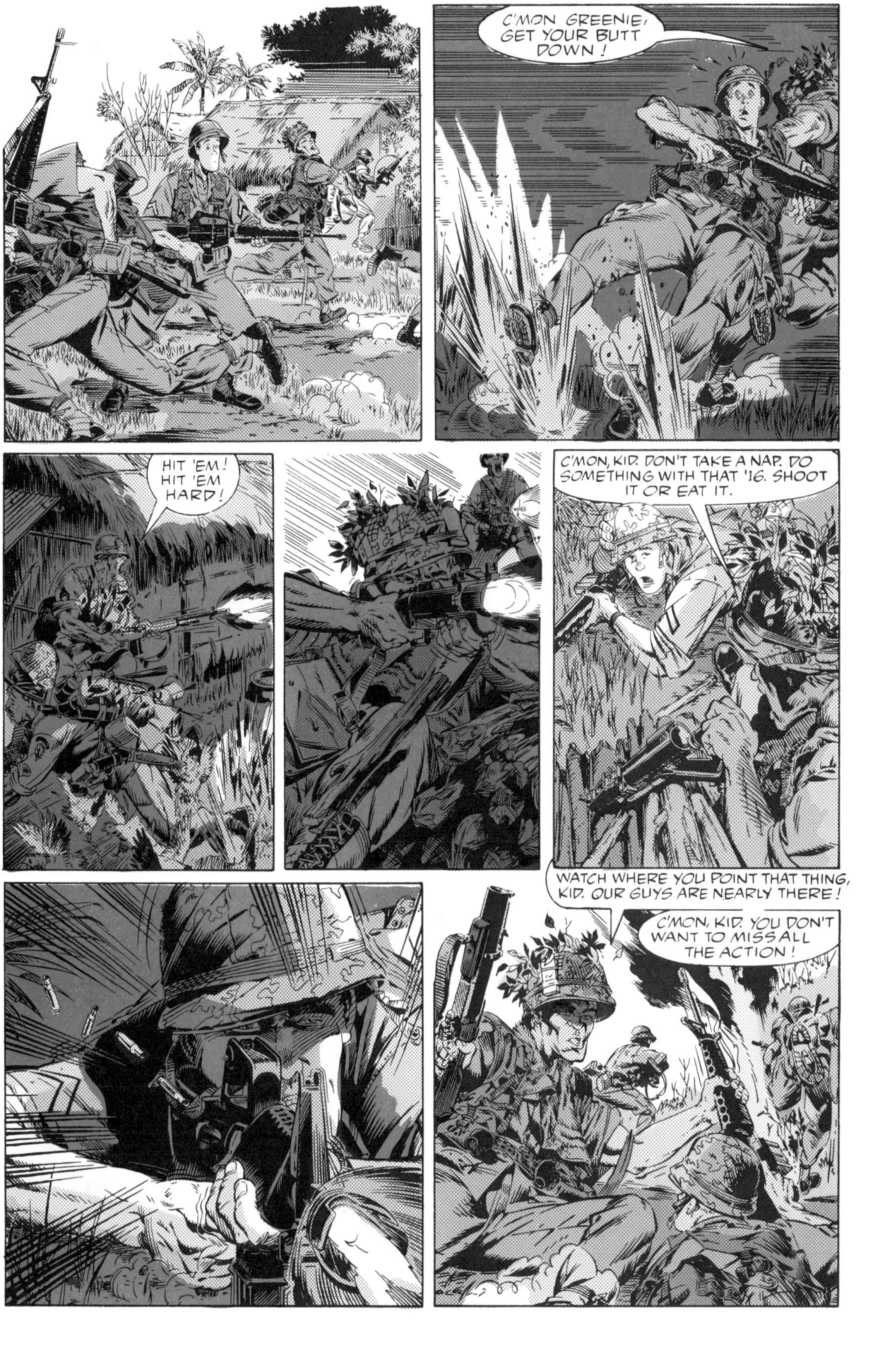
C'MON GREENIE, GET YOUR BUTT DOWN!
HIT 'EM! HIT 'EM HARD!
C'MON, KID. DON'T TAKE A NAP. DO SOMETHING WITH THAT '16. SHOOT IT OR EAT IT.
WATCH WHERE YOU POINT THAT THING, KID. OUR GUYS ARE NEARLY THERE!
C'MON, KID. YOU DON'T WANT TO MISS ALL THE ACTION!

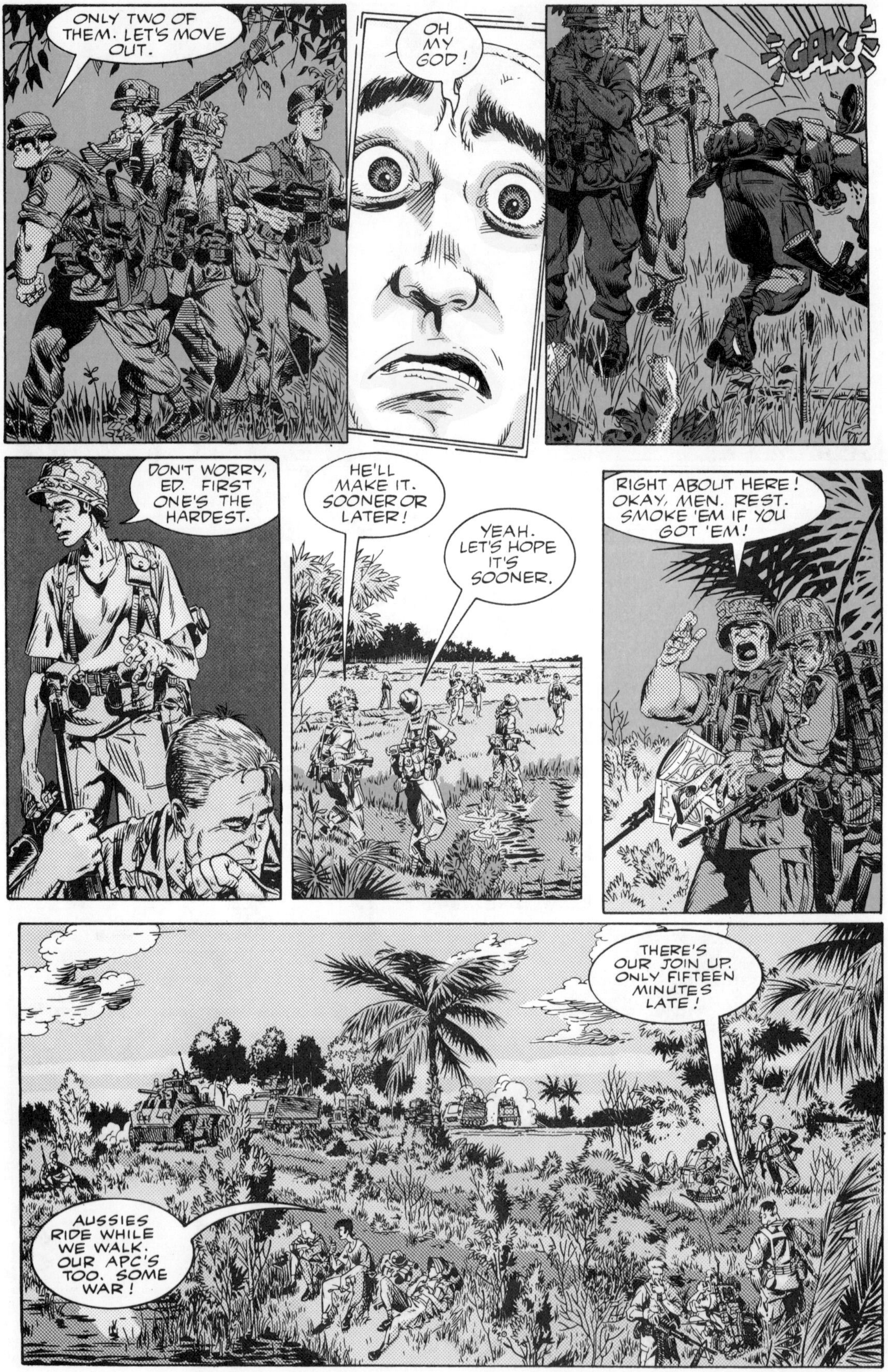
ONLY TWO OF THEM. LET'S MOVE OUT.
OH MY GOD!
GAK!
DON'T WORRY, ED. FIRST ONE'S THE HARDEST.
HE'LL MAKE IT. SOONER OR LATER!
YEAH. LET'S HOPE IT'S SOONER.
RIGHT ABOUT HERE! OKAY, MEN. REST. SMOKE 'EM IF YOU GOT 'EM!
THERE'S OUR JOIN UP. ONLY FIFTEEN MINUTES LATE!
AUSSIES RIDE WHILE WE WALK. OUR APC'S TOO. SOME WAR!

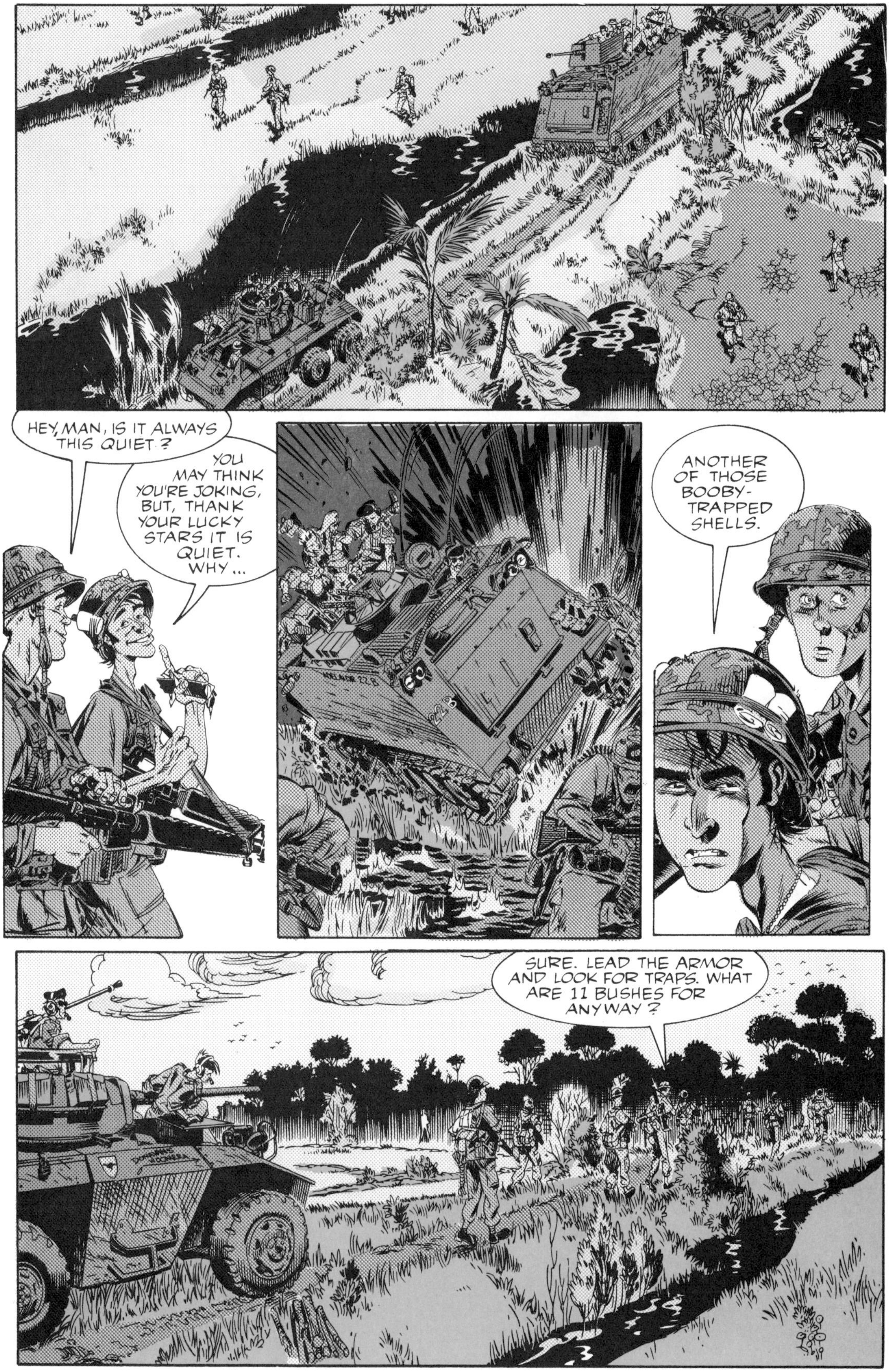
HEY, MAN, IS IT ALWAYS THIS QUIET?
YOU MAY THINK YOU'RE JOKING, BUT, THANK YOUR LUCKY STARS IT IS QUIET. WHY...
ANOTHER OF THOSE BOOBY-TRAPPED SHELLS.
SURE. LEAD THE ARMOR AND LOOK FOR TRAPS. WHAT ARE 11 BUSHES FOR ANYWAY?

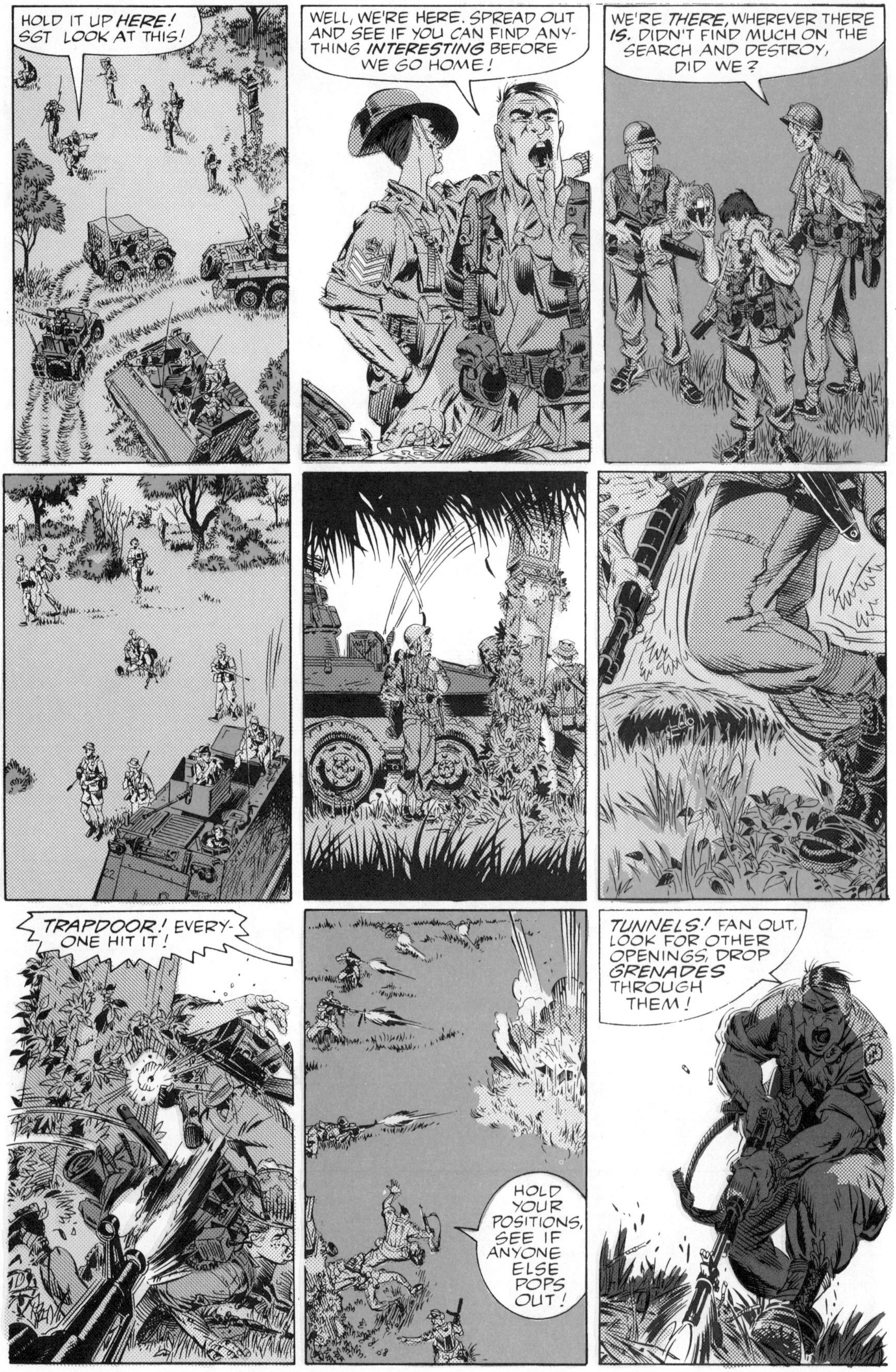
HOLD IT UP HERE! SGT LOOK AT THIS!
WELL, WE'RE HERE. SPREAD OUT AND SEE IF YOU CAN FIND ANYTHING INTERESTING BEFORE WE GO HOME!
WE'RE THERE, WHEREVER THERE IS. DIDN'T FIND MUCH ON THE SEARCH AND DESTROY, DID WE?
TRAPDOOR! EVERYONE HIT IT!
HOLD YOUR POSITIONS, SEE IF ANYONE ELSE POPS OUT!
TUNNELS! FAN OUT, LOOK FOR OTHER OPENINGS, DROP GRENADES THROUGH THEM!

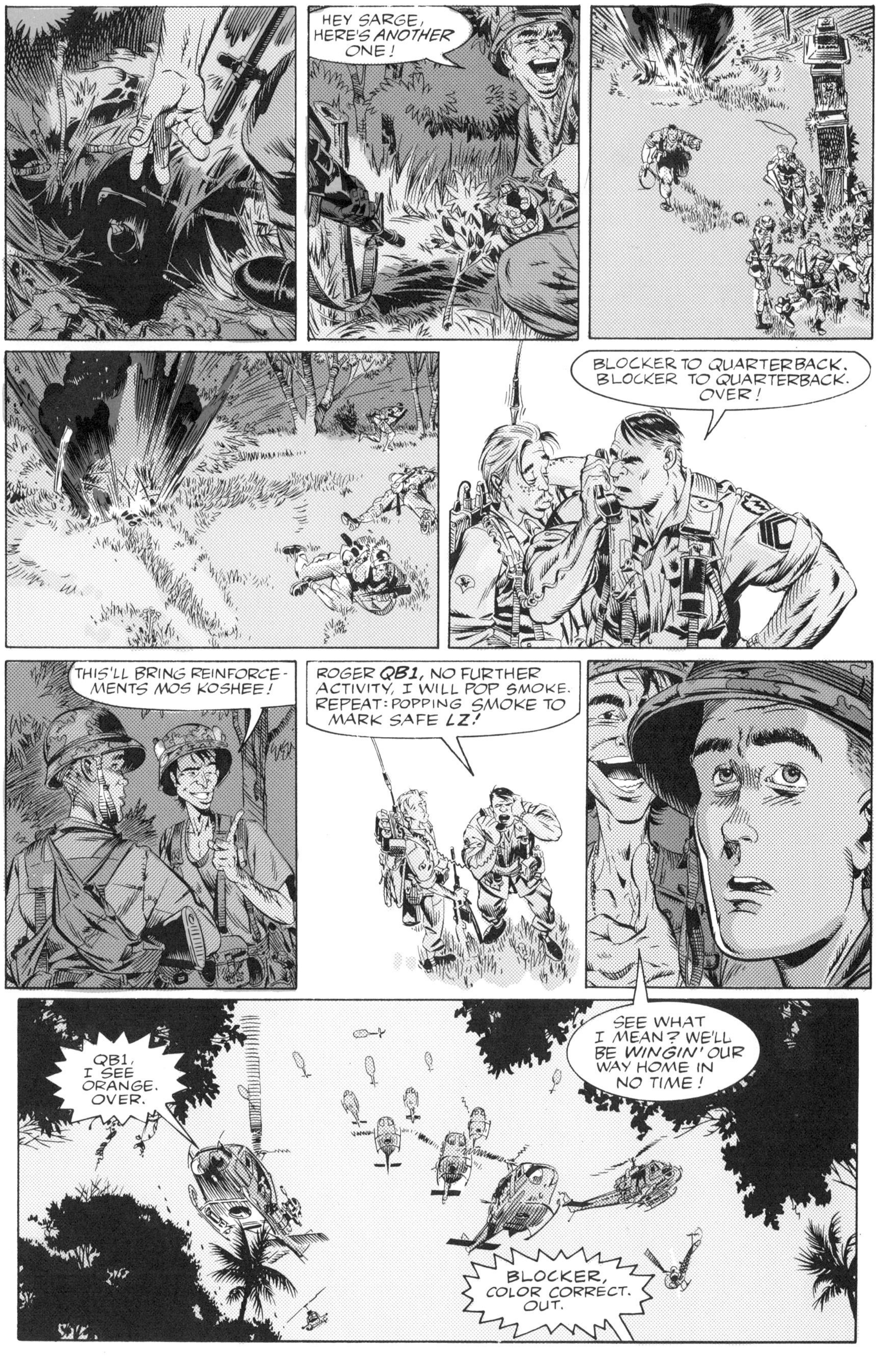
HEY SARGE, HERE'S ANOTHER ONE!
BLOCKER TO QUARTERBACK. BLOCKER TO QUARTERBACK. OVER!
THIS'LL BRING REINFORCE-MENTS MOS KOSHEE!
ROGER QB1, NO FURTHER ACTIVITY, I WILL POP SMOKE. REPEAT: POPPING SMOKE TO MARK SAFE LZ!
SEE WHAT I MEAN? WE'LL BE WINGIN' OUR WAY HOME IN NO TIME!
QB1, I SEE ORANGE. OVER.
BLOCKER, COLOR CORRECT. OUT.

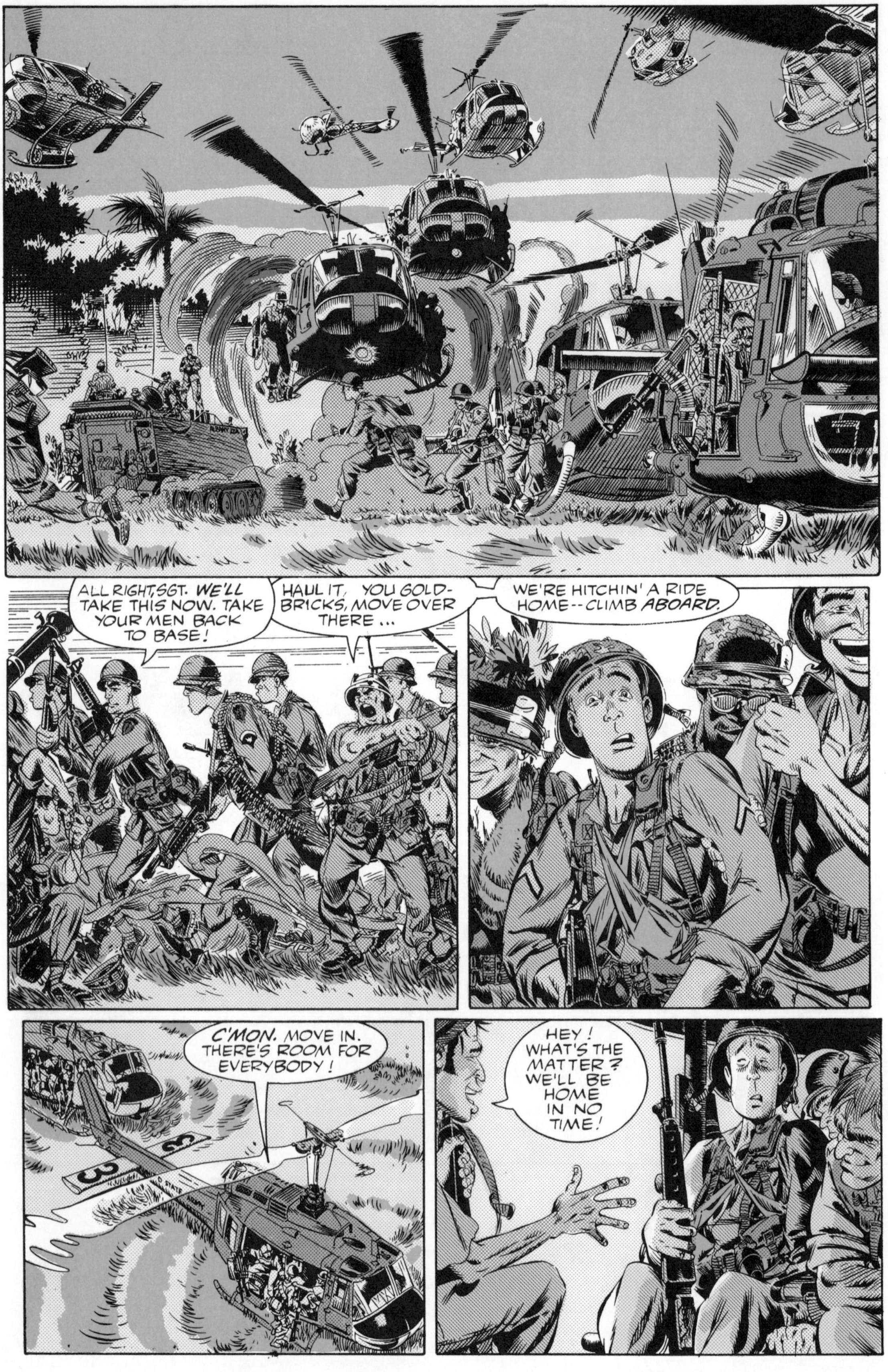
ALL RIGHT, SGT. *WE'LL* TAKE THIS NOW. TAKE YOUR MEN BACK TO BASE!
HAUL IT, YOU GOLD-BRICKS, MOVE OVER THERE...
WE'RE HITCHIN' A RIDE HOME--CLIMB *ABOARD.*
C'MON. MOVE IN. THERE'S ROOM FOR EVERYBODY!
HEY! WHAT'S THE MATTER? WE'LL BE HOME IN NO TIME!

I...I HAVE THIS *PROBLEM* WITH HEIGHTS!

YOU'D BETTER GET *OVER* IT. WE RIDE THESE BIRDS *EVERYWHERE!*

YEAH, GET USED TO IT!

LATER...

WELL, BOY, YOU MADE IT. YOU'VE HAD YOUR FIRST TASTE OF *COMBAT!* YOU'RE A *VET!* HOW DOES IT FEEL?

HOME OF THE
4/23 INFANTRY
MECHANIZED, OF COURSE
TOMAHAWKS

I DON'T KNOW YET, I'M STILL A LITTLE *NUMB!*

DON'T WORRY, YOU'LL GET MORE NUMB THAN THIS!

LET'S HAT-UP AND BLOW THIS PLACE! LET'S GO TO THE *MOVIE...* I HEAR THEY GOT A GOOD ONE!

LOOK AT THIS *CRUD.* CAN YOU BELIEVE IT?!

NOBODY'S GOT ANY *COVER!* THEY'D *ALL* GET *KILLED!*

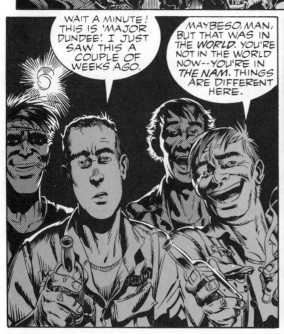

WAIT A MINUTE! THIS IS 'MAJOR DUNDEE'. I JUST SAW THIS A COUPLE OF WEEKS AGO.

MAYBE SO, MAN, BUT THAT WAS IN *THE WORLD.* YOU'RE NOT IN THE *WORLD* NOW--YOU'RE IN *THE NAM.* THINGS ARE DIFFERENT HERE.

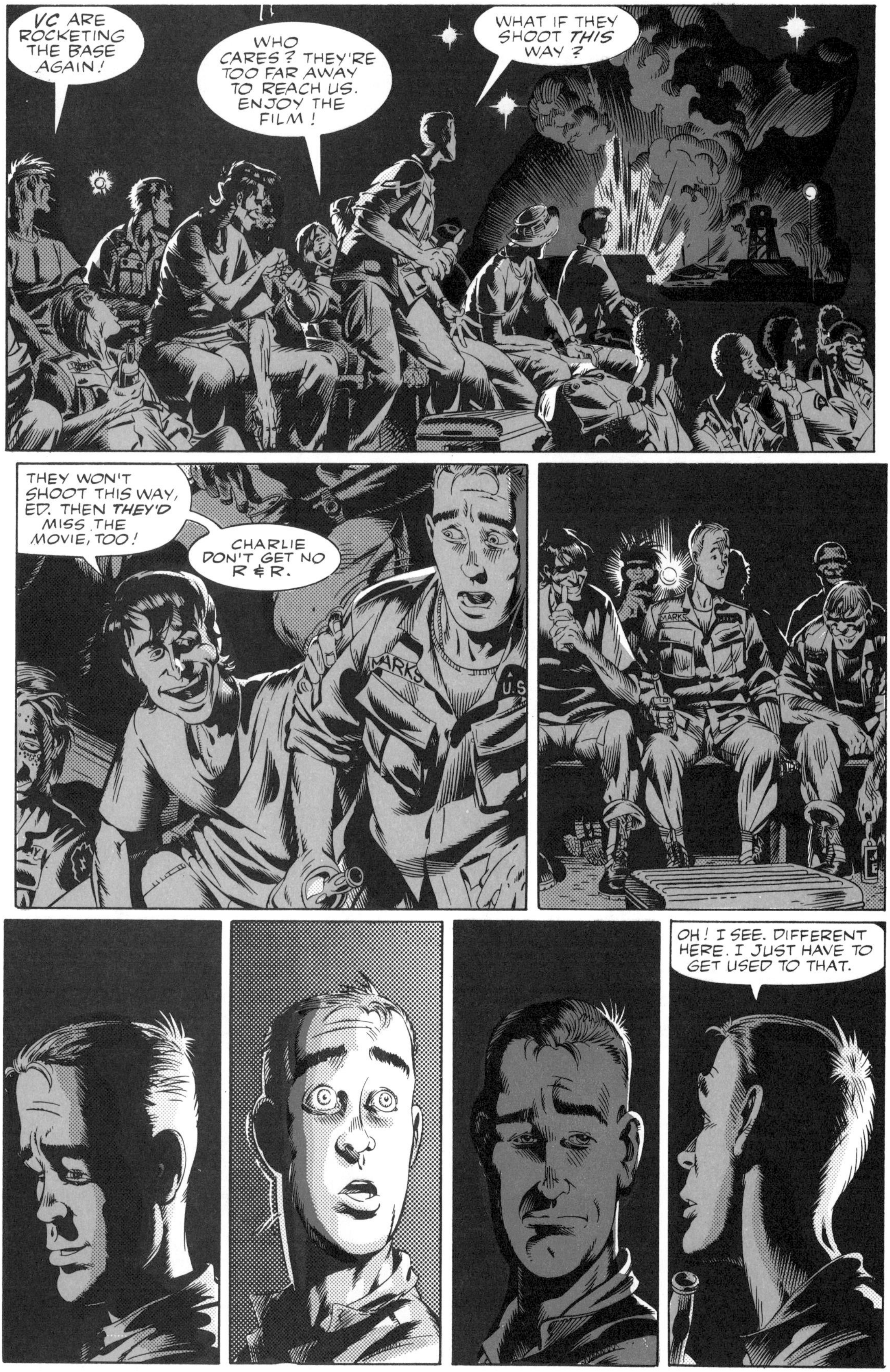
VC ARE ROCKETING THE BASE AGAIN!
WHO CARES? THEY'RE TOO FAR AWAY TO REACH US. ENJOY THE FILM!
WHAT IF THEY SHOOT THIS WAY?
THEY WON'T SHOOT THIS WAY, ED. THEN THEY'D MISS THE MOVIE, TOO!
CHARLIE DON'T GET NO R & R.
MARKS
U.S
MARKS
OH! I SEE. DIFFERENT HERE. I JUST HAVE TO GET USED TO THAT.

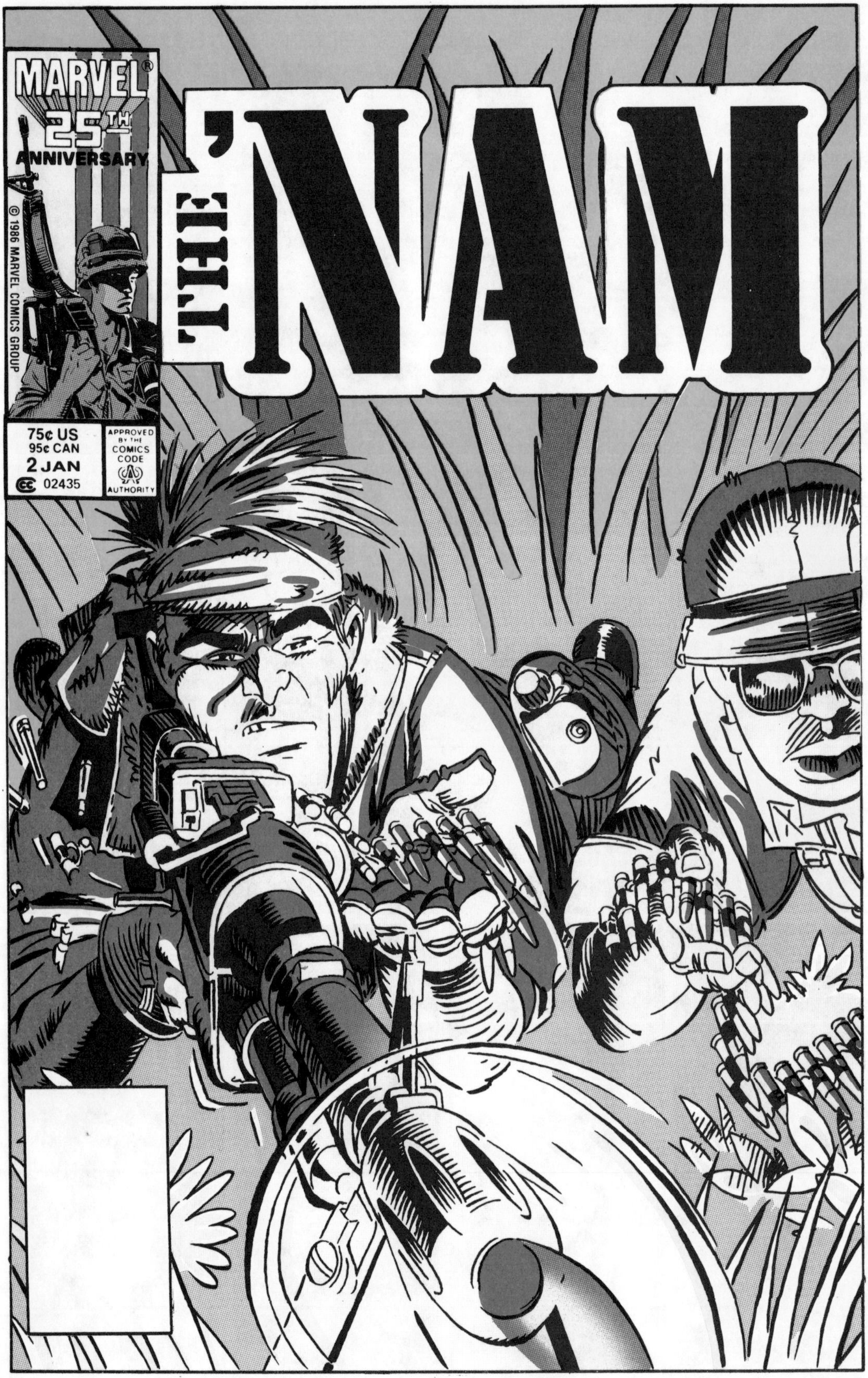
MARVEL®
25TH
ANNIVERSARY
© 1986 MARVEL COMICS GROUP
THE 'NAM
75¢ US
95¢ CAN
2 JAN
02435
APPROVED BY THE COMICS CODE AUTHORITY

Stan Lee PRESENTS: THE 'NAM™

DOUG MURRAY — WRITER.
MICHAEL GOLDEN — PENCILER.
ARMANDO GIL — INKER.
PHIL FELIX — LETTERER AND COLORIST.
LARRY HAMA — EDITOR.
JAMES SHOOTER — EDITOR IN CHIEF.

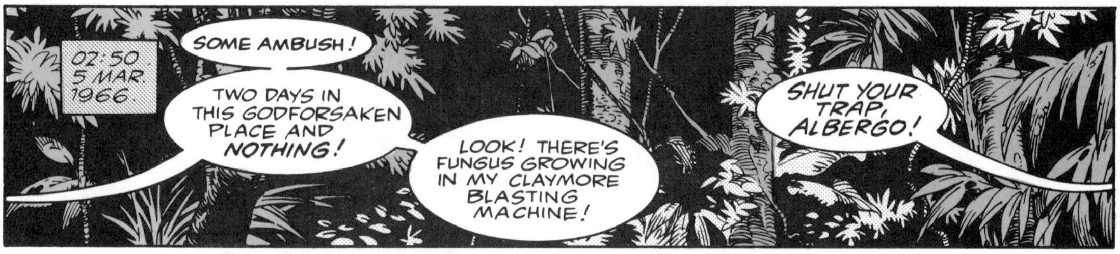
02:50 5 MAR. 1966.
SOME AMBUSH!
TWO DAYS IN THIS GODFORSAKEN PLACE AND NOTHING!
LOOK! THERE'S FUNGUS GROWING IN MY CLAYMORE BLASTING MACHINE!
SHUT YOUR TRAP, ALBERGO!

"DUSTOFF"

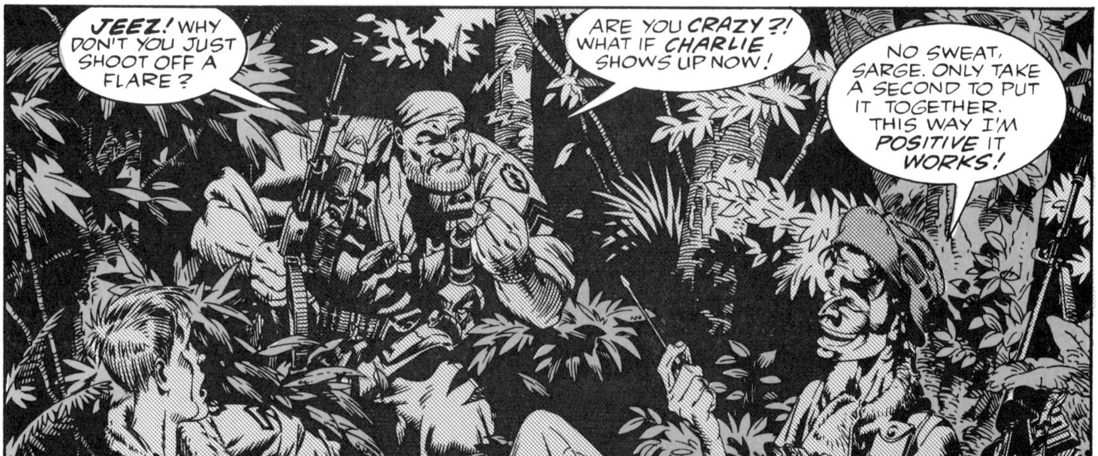
JEEZ! WHY DON'T YOU JUST SHOOT OFF A FLARE?
ARE YOU CRAZY?! WHAT IF CHARLIE SHOWS UP NOW!
NO SWEAT, SARGE. ONLY TAKE A SECOND TO PUT IT TOGETHER. THIS WAY I'M POSITIVE IT WORKS!

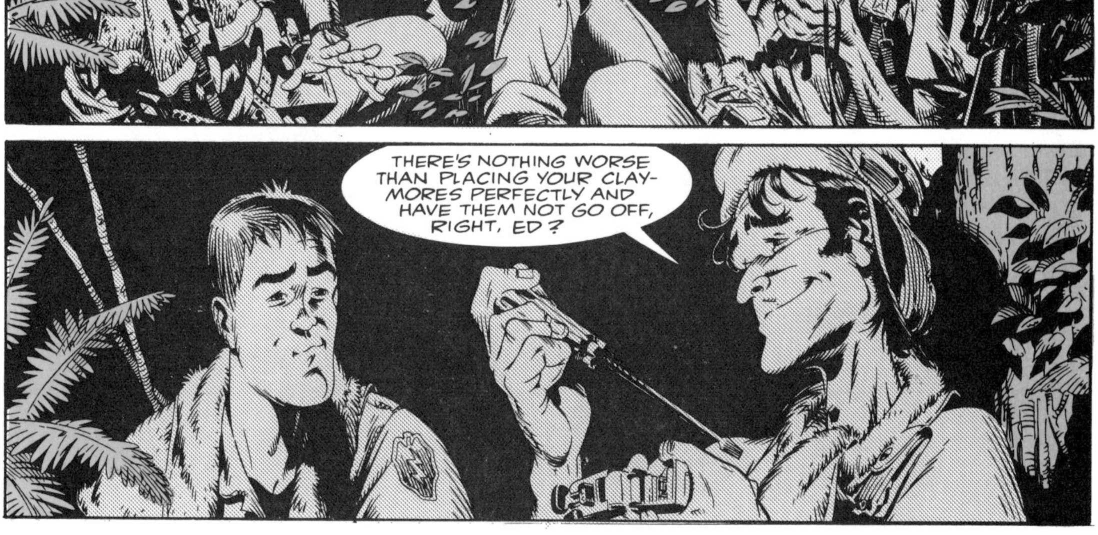
THERE'S NOTHING WORSE THAN PLACING YOUR CLAYMORES PERFECTLY AND HAVE THEM NOT GO OFF, RIGHT, ED?

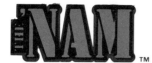

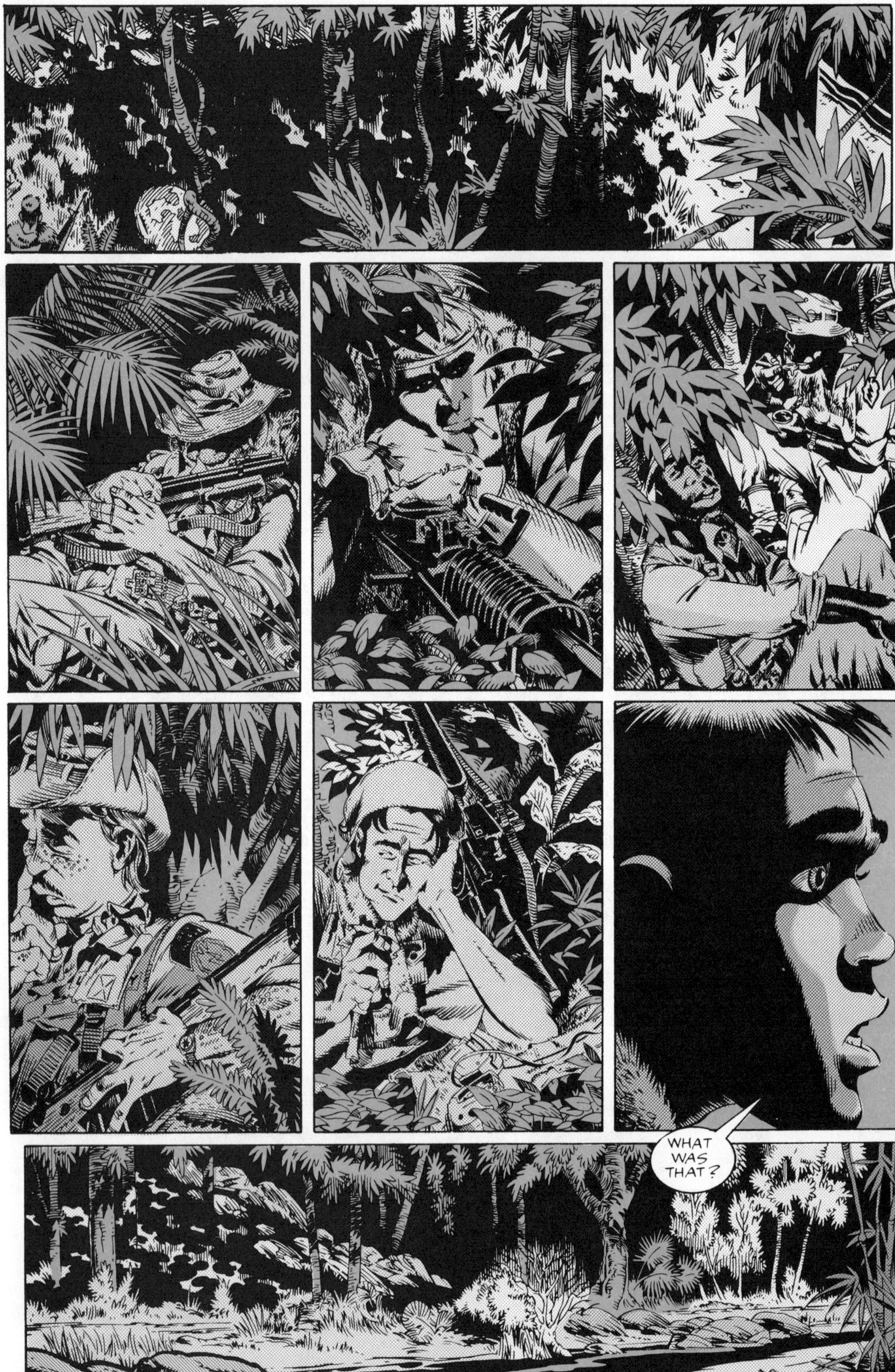
WHAT WAS THAT?

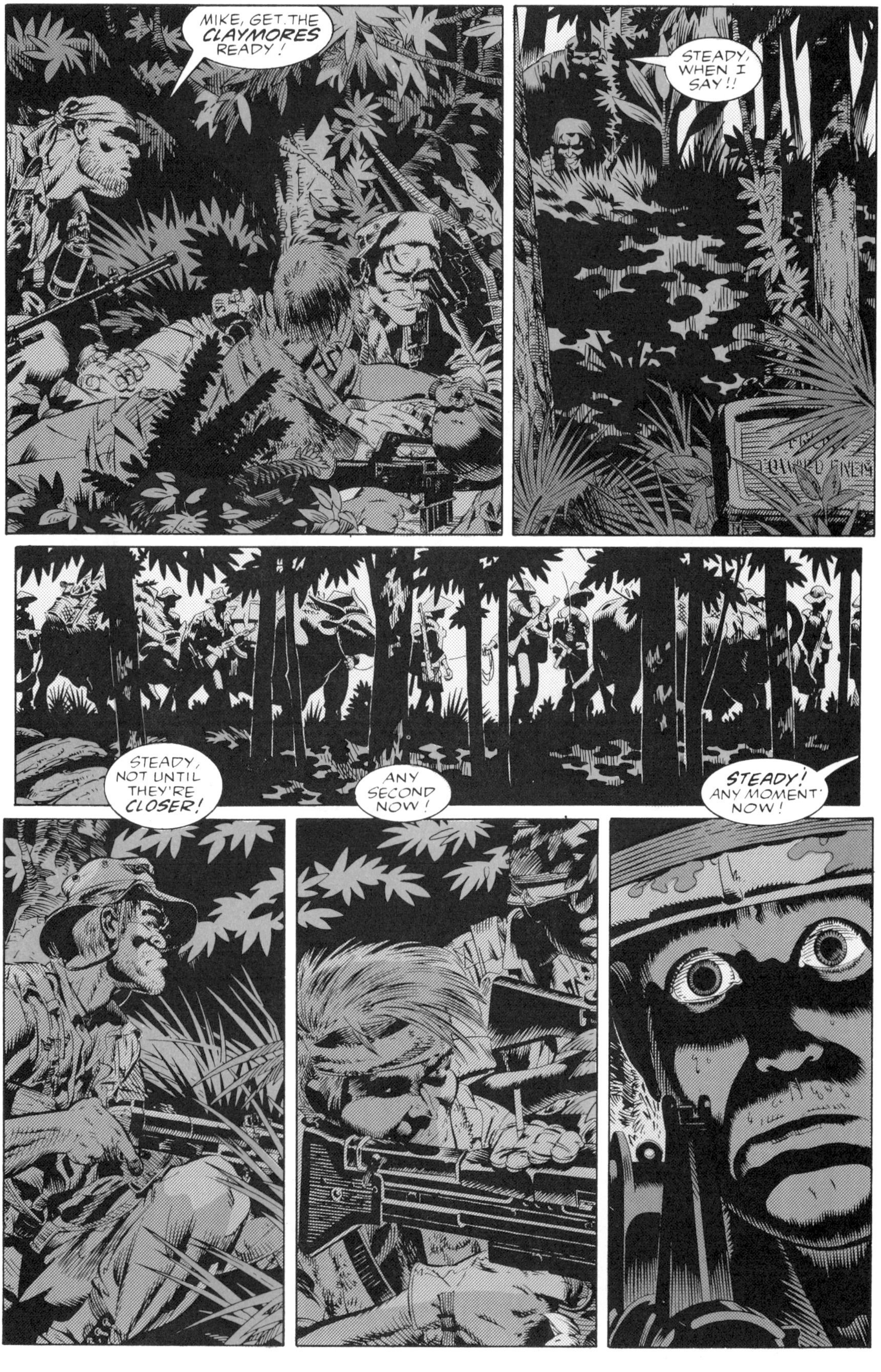
MIKE, GET THE **CLAYMORES** READY!
STEADY, WHEN I SAY!!
STEADY, NOT UNTIL THEY'RE **CLOSER**!
ANY SECOND NOW!
STEADY! ANY MOMENT NOW!

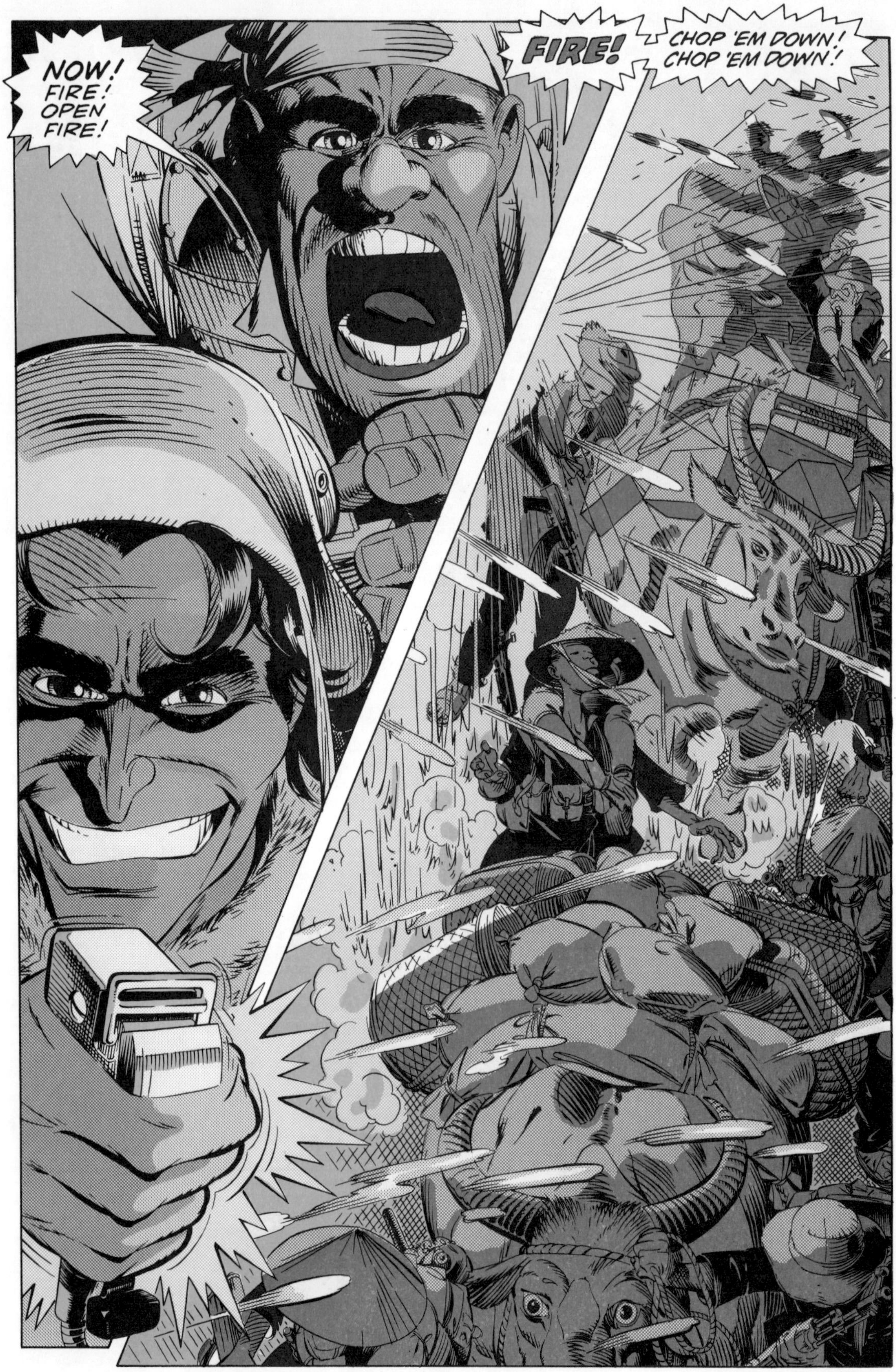
NOW! FIRE! OPEN FIRE!
FIRE!
CHOP 'EM DOWN! CHOP 'EM DOWN!

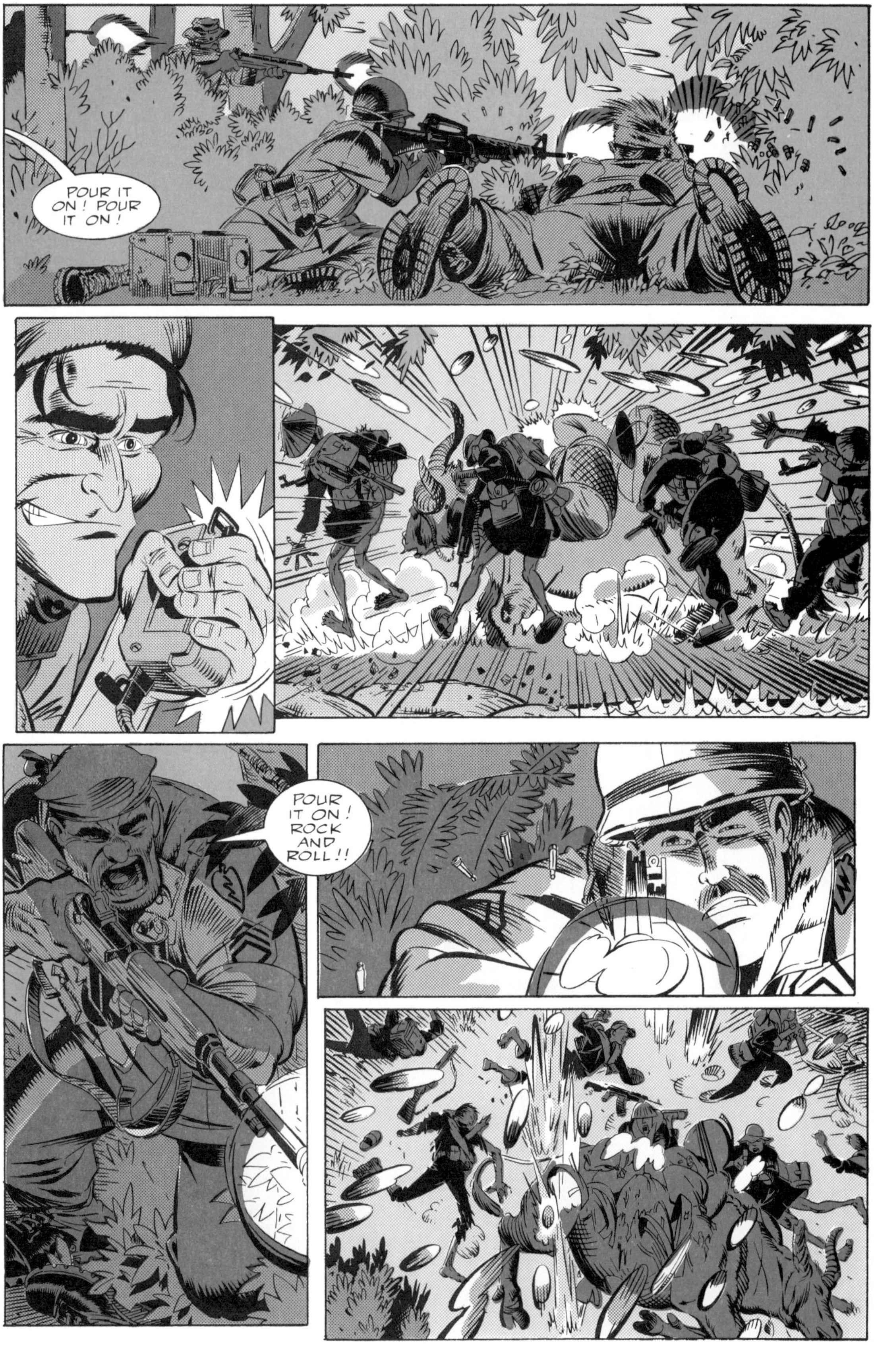
POUR IT ON! POUR IT ON!
POUR IT ON! ROCK AND ROLL!!

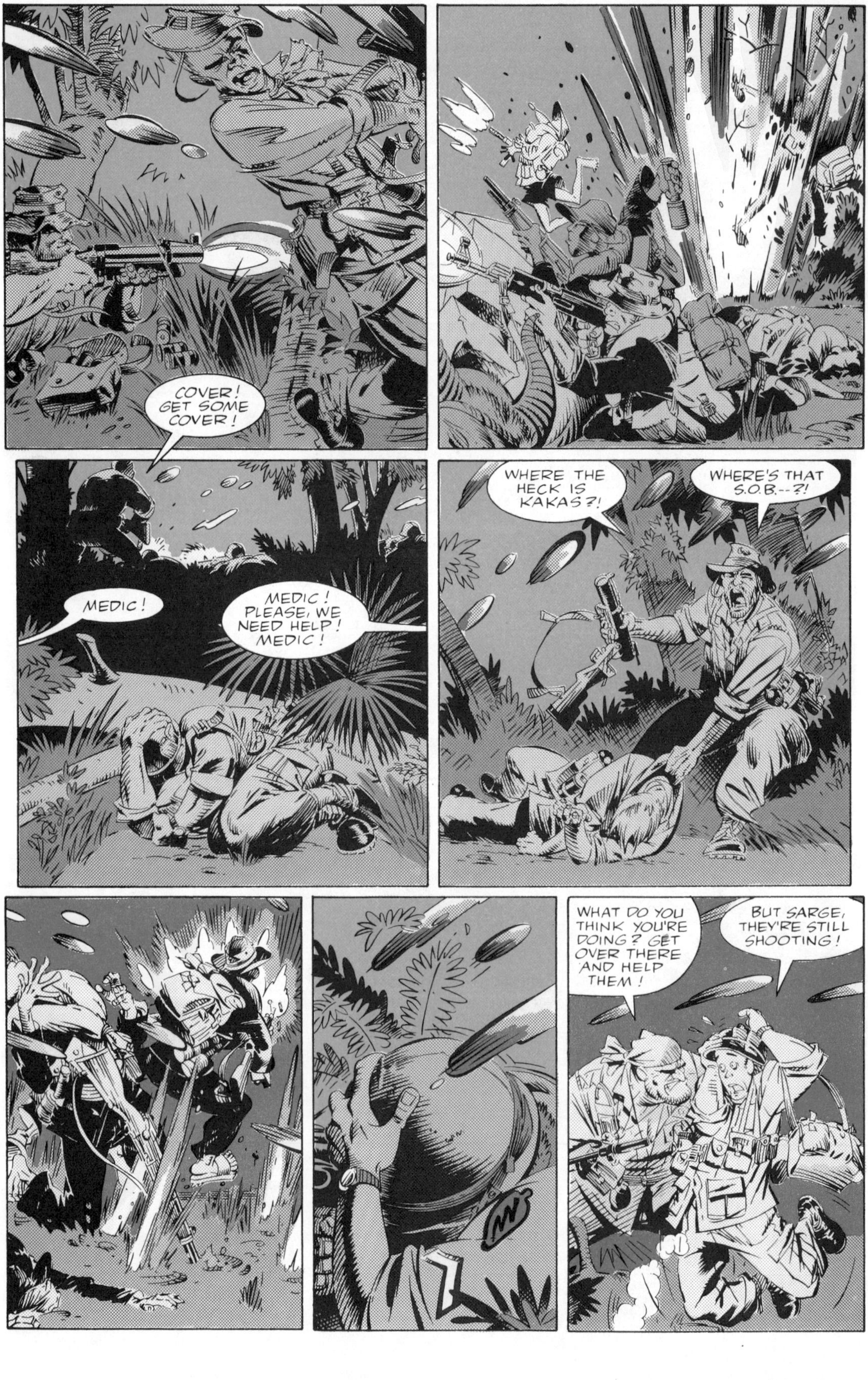
COVER! GET SOME COVER!
MEDIC!
MEDIC! PLEASE, WE NEED HELP! MEDIC!
WHERE THE HECK IS KAKAS?!
WHERE'S THAT S.O.B.--?!
WHAT DO YOU THINK YOU'RE DOING? GET OVER THERE AND HELP THEM!
BUT SARGE, THEY'RE STILL SHOOTING!

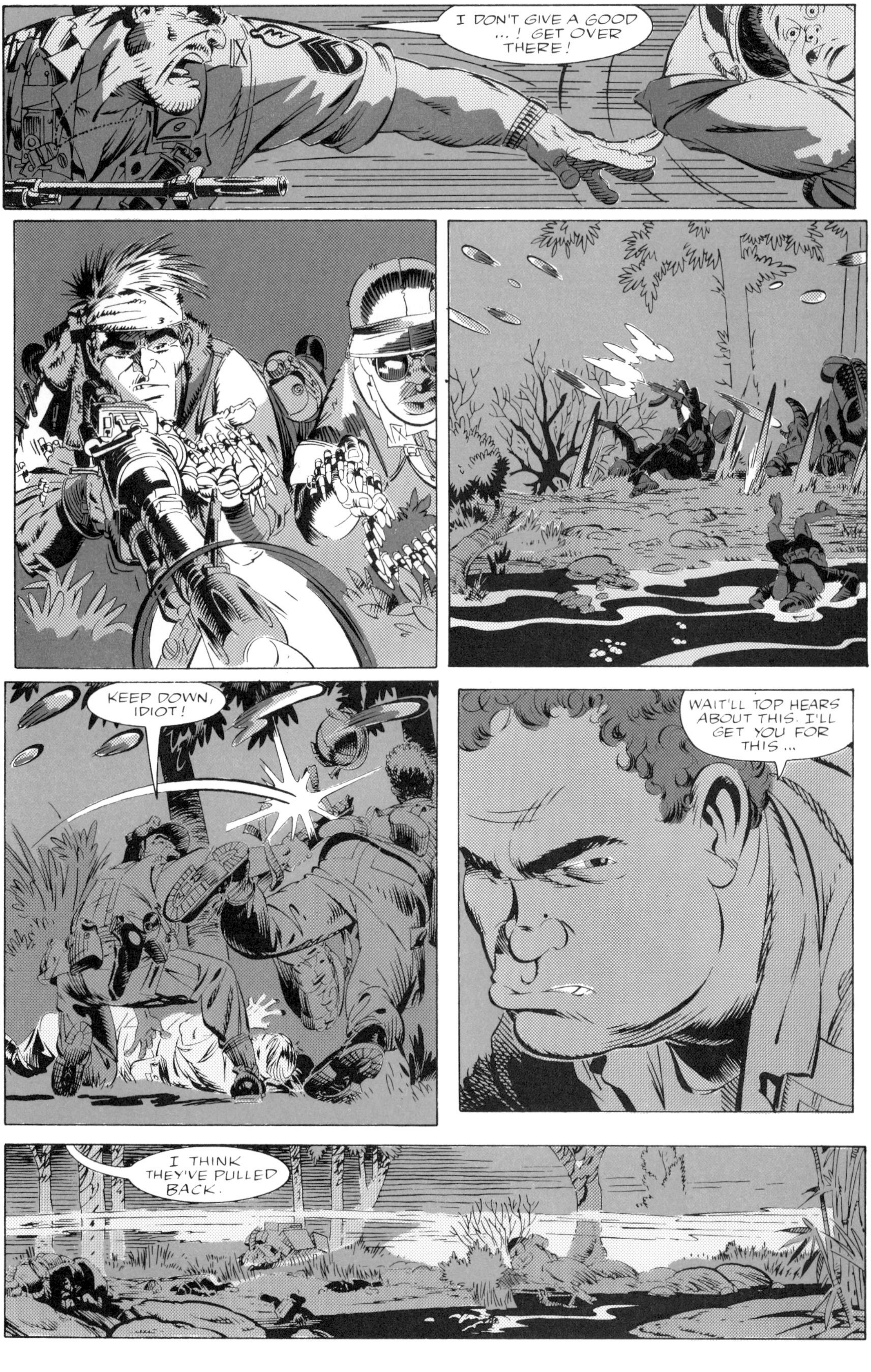
I DON'T GIVE A GOOD ... ! GET OVER THERE!
KEEP DOWN, IDIOT!
WAIT'LL TOP HEARS ABOUT THIS. I'LL GET YOU FOR THIS...
I THINK THEY'VE PULLED BACK.

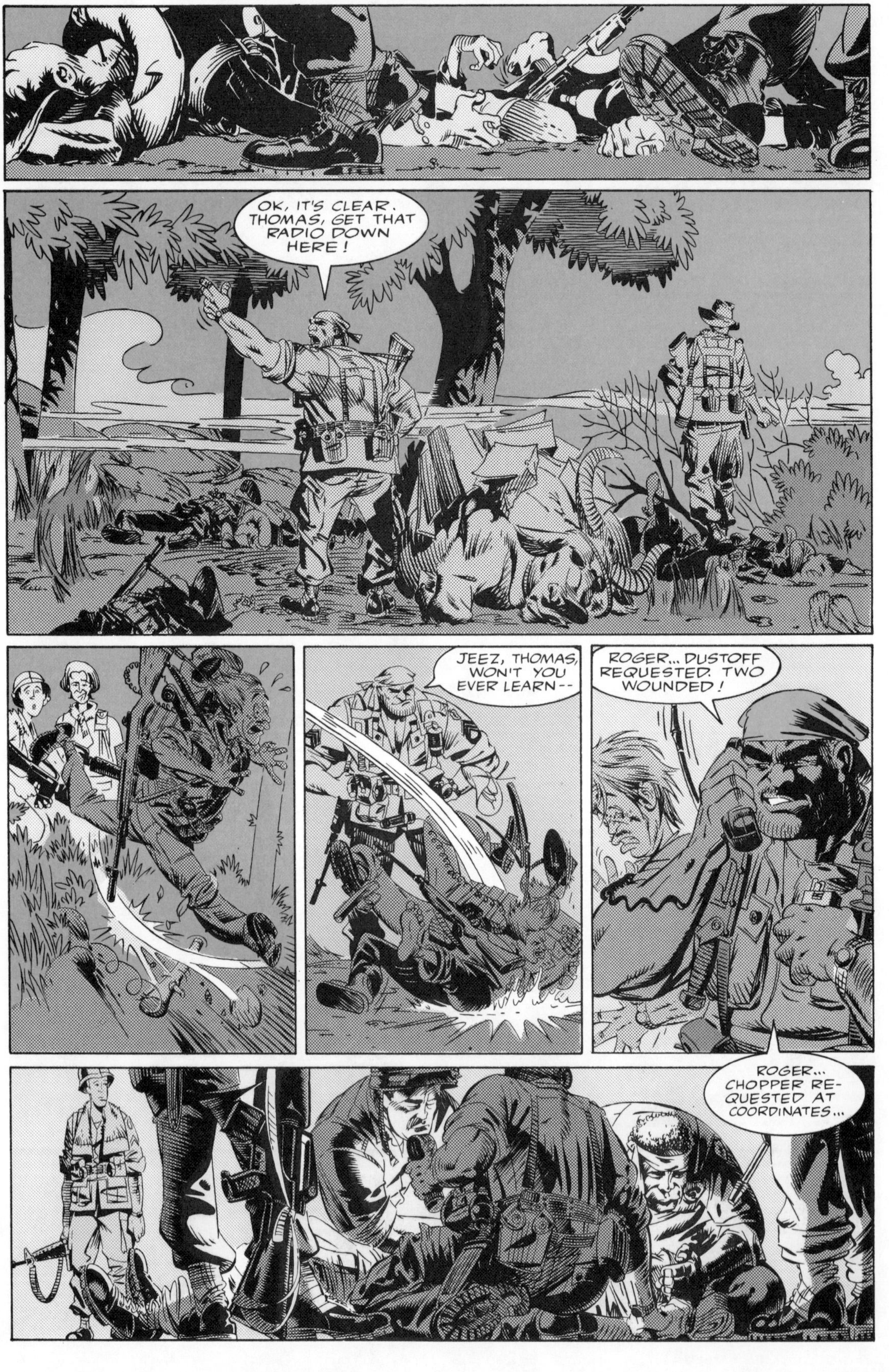
OK, IT'S CLEAR. THOMAS, GET THAT RADIO DOWN HERE!
JEEZ, THOMAS, WON'T YOU EVER LEARN--
ROGER... DUSTOFF REQUESTED. TWO WOUNDED!
ROGER... CHOPPER RE-QUESTED AT COORDINATES...

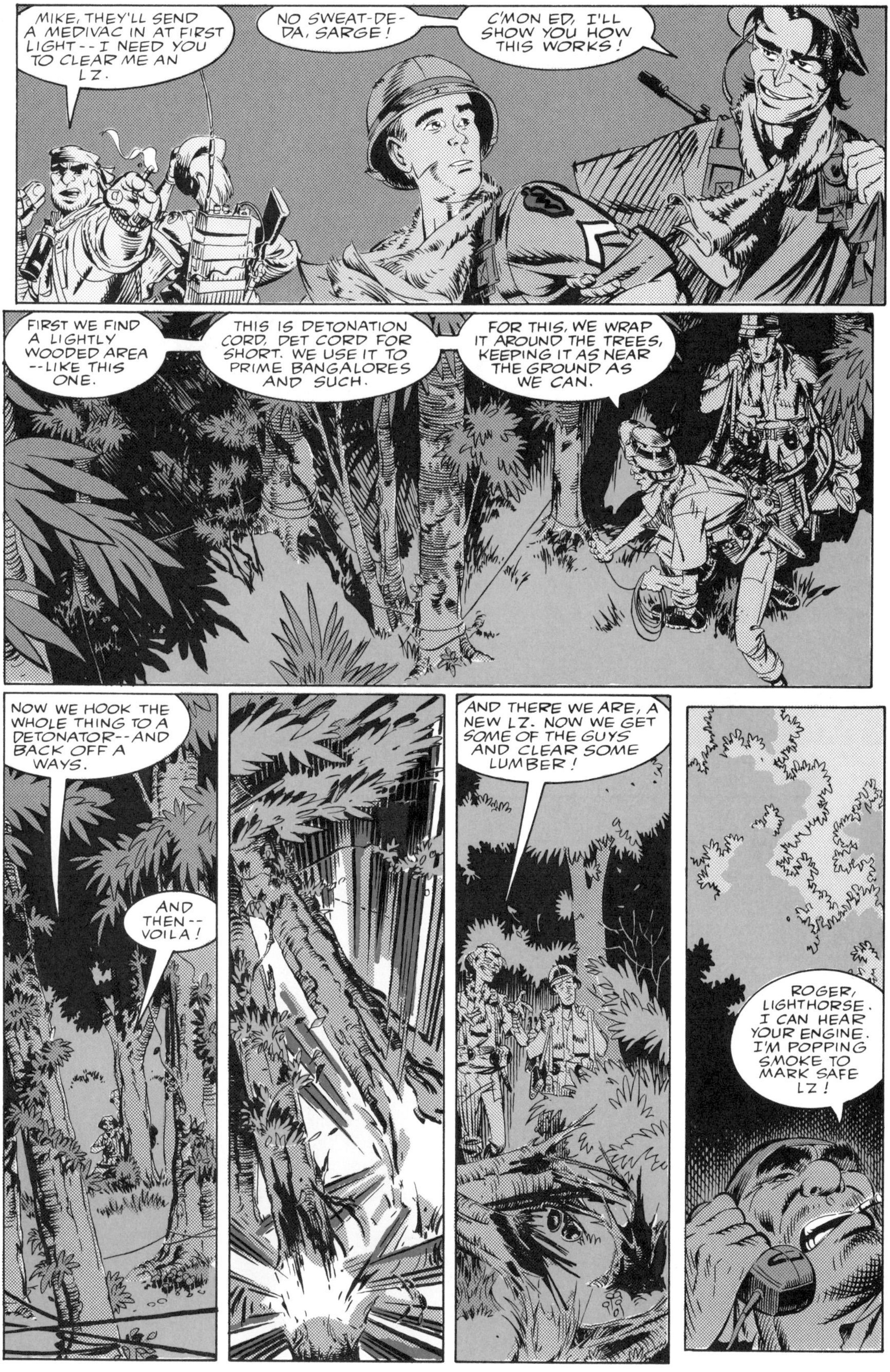
MIKE, THEY'LL SEND A MEDIVAC IN AT FIRST LIGHT--I NEED YOU TO CLEAR ME AN LZ.
NO SWEAT-DE-DA, SARGE!
C'MON ED, I'LL SHOW YOU HOW THIS WORKS!
FIRST WE FIND A LIGHTLY WOODED AREA --LIKE THIS ONE.
THIS IS DETONATION CORD, DET CORD FOR SHORT. WE USE IT TO PRIME BANGALORES AND SUCH.
FOR THIS, WE WRAP IT AROUND THE TREES, KEEPING IT AS NEAR THE GROUND AS WE CAN.
NOW WE HOOK THE WHOLE THING TO A DETONATOR--AND BACK OFF A WAYS.
AND THEN--VOILA!
AND THERE WE ARE, A NEW LZ. NOW WE GET SOME OF THE GUYS AND CLEAR SOME LUMBER!
ROGER, LIGHTHORSE. I CAN HEAR YOUR ENGINE. I'M POPPING SMOKE TO MARK SAFE LZ!

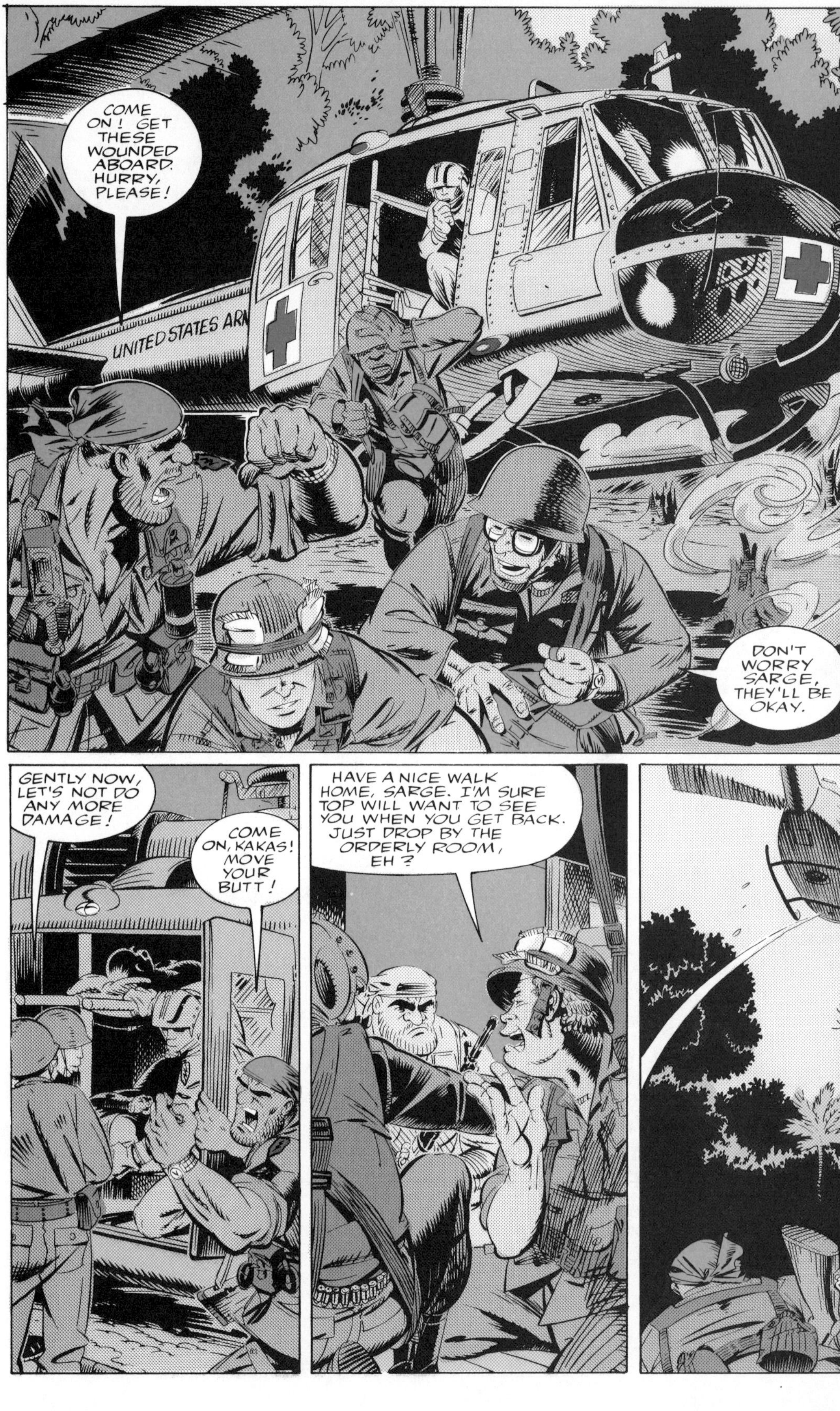
COME ON! GET THESE WOUNDED ABOARD. HURRY, PLEASE!
UNITED STATES ARM
DON'T WORRY SARGE, THEY'LL BE OKAY.
GENTLY NOW, LET'S NOT DO ANY MORE DAMAGE!
COME ON, KAKAS! MOVE YOUR BUTT!
HAVE A NICE WALK HOME, SARGE. I'M SURE TOP WILL WANT TO SEE YOU WHEN YOU GET BACK. JUST DROP BY THE ORDERLY ROOM, EH?

ALL RIGHT, PICK UP THE JUNK. LET'S GO HOME.

SOME BATTALION! TOO CHEAP TO SEND A CHOPPER OUT FOR US!

THAT KAKAS! I'LL STOP BY THE ORDERLY ROOM ALL RIGHT, AND WHEN I DO...

LOOKS LIKE THE SARGE THINKS KAKAS IS GONNA MAKE TROUBLE!

HOME OF THE 4/23 INFANTRY MECHANIZED OF COURSE

WHAT KIND OF TROUBLE COULD HE MAKE?

O.K. BOYS, GRAB A SHOWER AND GET SOME SLEEP.

HE'S TIGHT WITH TOP. JUST ABOUT ANY KIND HE WANTED.

MAN, I COULD SLEEP FOR TWO DAYS.

YEAH, ME, TOO!

HEADQUARTERS 4/23 INFANTRY

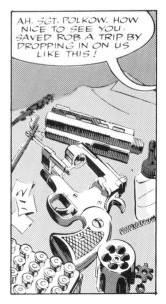

AH, SGT. POLKOW. HOW NICE TO SEE YOU. SAVED ROB A TRIP BY DROPPING IN ON US LIKE THIS!

WHAT DO YOU WANT, TOP?!

I CAN SEE YOUR LAPDOG'S BEEN HERE TO SEE YOU.

YOU MEAN SPECIALIST KAKAS? HE DID MENTION THAT YOU UN-WARRANTLY EXPOSED HIM TO ENEMY FIRE. BUT THAT IS UNIMPORTANT.

ORDERLY ROOM

UNIMPORTANT? THEN WHY...

QUITE UNIMPORTANT! HOWEVER, I DO HAVE SOMETHING IMPORTANT TO SPEAK TO YOU OF. SOMETHING QUITE IMPORTANT, A MISSION!

MISSION! NOW? MY BOYS JUST GOT BACK FROM THREE DAYS IN THE FIELD! THEY'RE NOT GOIN' ON ANOTHER...

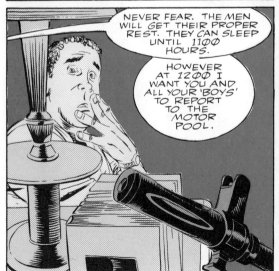

NEVER FEAR. THE MEN WILL GET THEIR PROPER REST. THEY CAN SLEEP UNTIL 1100 HOURS.

HOWEVER AT 1200 I WANT YOU AND ALL YOUR 'BOYS' TO REPORT TO THE MOTOR POOL.

FOUR HOURS REST AFTER THREE DAYS IN THE FIELD! ARE YOU CRAZY?!

WHAT WOULD THE CAPTAIN SAY ABOUT THAT?!

YOU CAN TALK TO THE CAPTAIN IF YOU LIKE, OF COURSE! HOWEVER, KNOWING HIM AS I DO, I DOUBT HE'LL APPRECIATE IT. REGULATIONS DO SAY FOUR HOURS REST A DAY, YOU KNOW. HOWEVER...

YOU WIN... FOR NOW. I'LL BE BACK TO TALK SOME MORE WHEN WE GET BACK! SEE YOU THEN, YOU SLIMY SLUG!

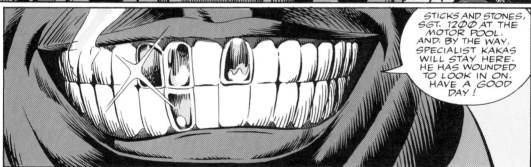

STICKS AND STONES, SGT. 1200 AT THE MOTOR POOL. AND, BY THE WAY, SPECIALIST KAKAS WILL STAY HERE. HE HAS WOUNDED TO LOOK IN ON. HAVE A GOOD DAY!

AND SO, AT 1200 HOURS...

LOOK AT IT THIS WAY, AT LEAST WE GET TO RIDE THIS TIME...

ALL RIGHT, MOUNT UP!

NOT IN THERE, KID. WE RIDE UP ON TOP!
US ARMY
WHY UP HERE INSTEAD OF IN THERE?
IN THERE, IF WE HIT A MINE, WE ALL GET TO BE INSTANT CHOPPED MEAT. UP HERE, WE GOT A CHANCE.
YOU SEE, THE ARMOR'S SO THIN ON THESE THINGS, SHRAPNEL JUST COMES IN AND BOUNCES AROUND.
BETTER TO BE ON TOP! TAKE THE SUN! GET A TAN!
HOME OF THE
4/23 INFANTRY
MECHANIZED, OF COURSE!
US ARMY

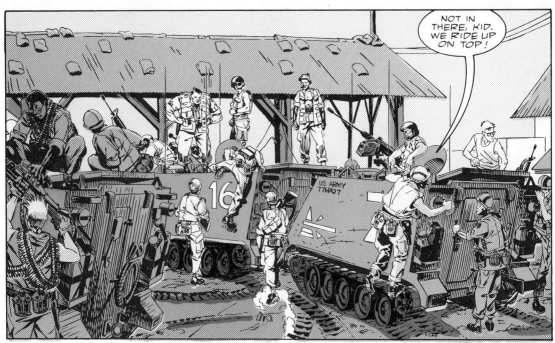

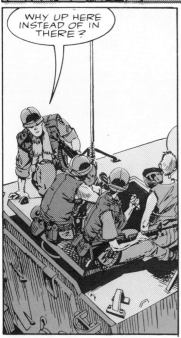

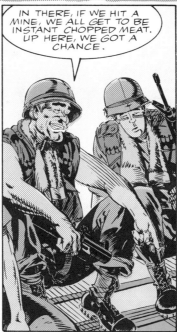

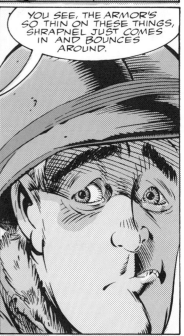

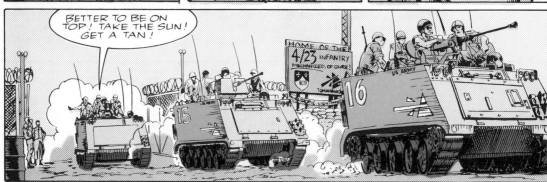

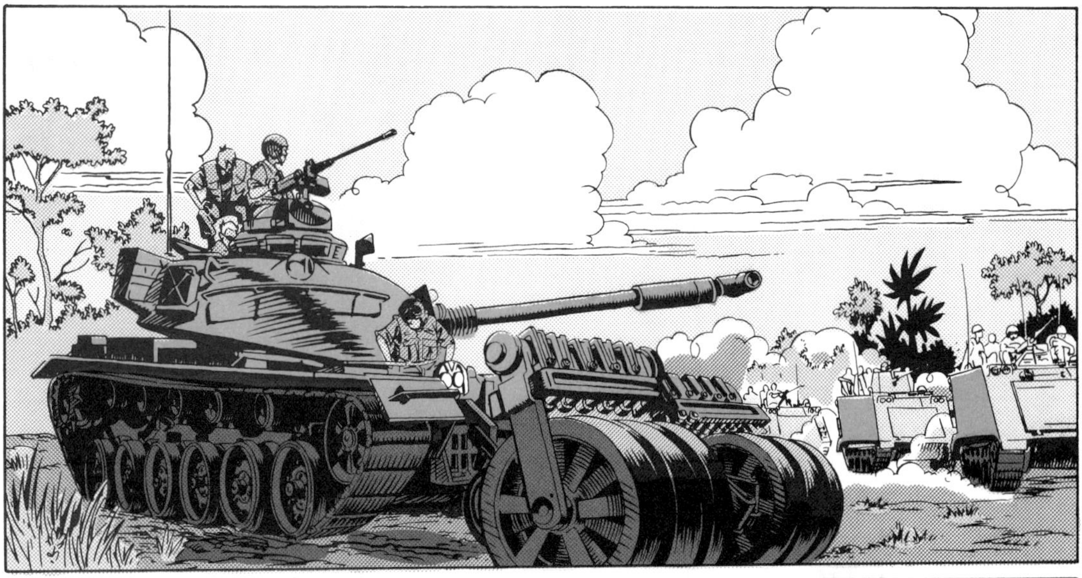

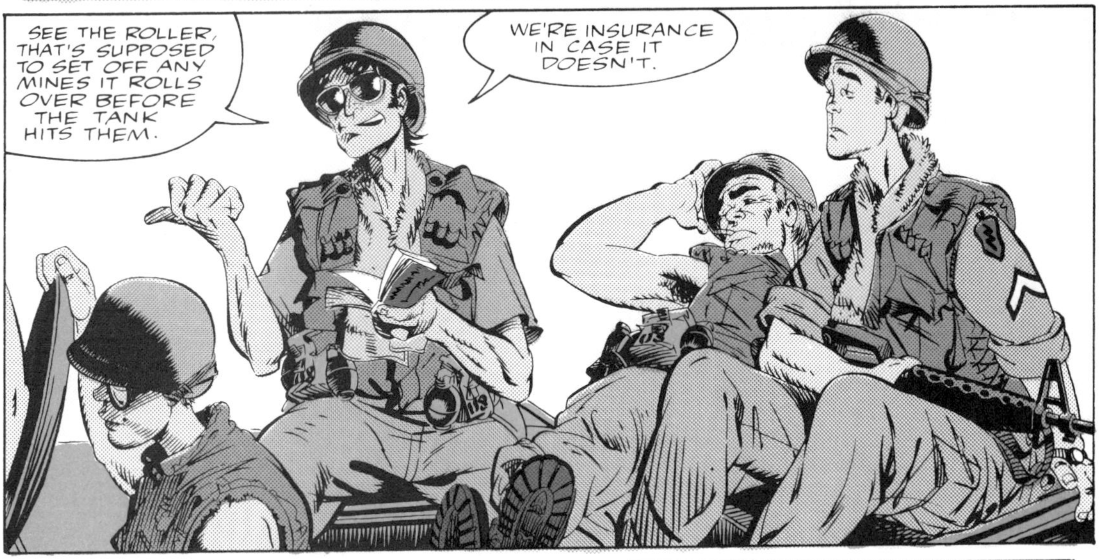
SEE THE ROLLER, THAT'S SUPPOSED TO SET OFF ANY MINES IT ROLLS OVER BEFORE THE TANK HITS THEM.
WE'RE INSURANCE IN CASE IT DOESN'T.

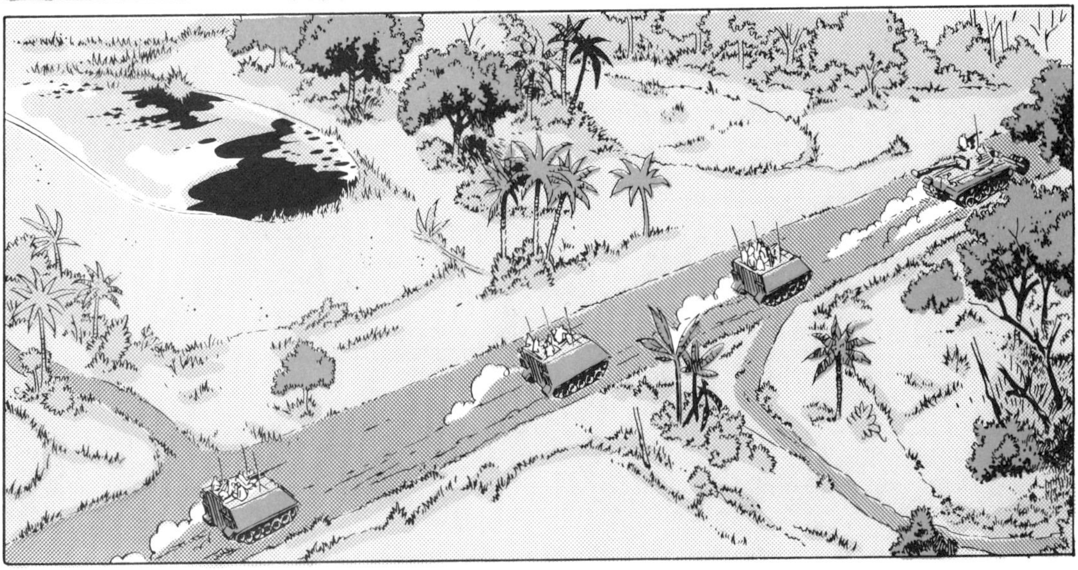

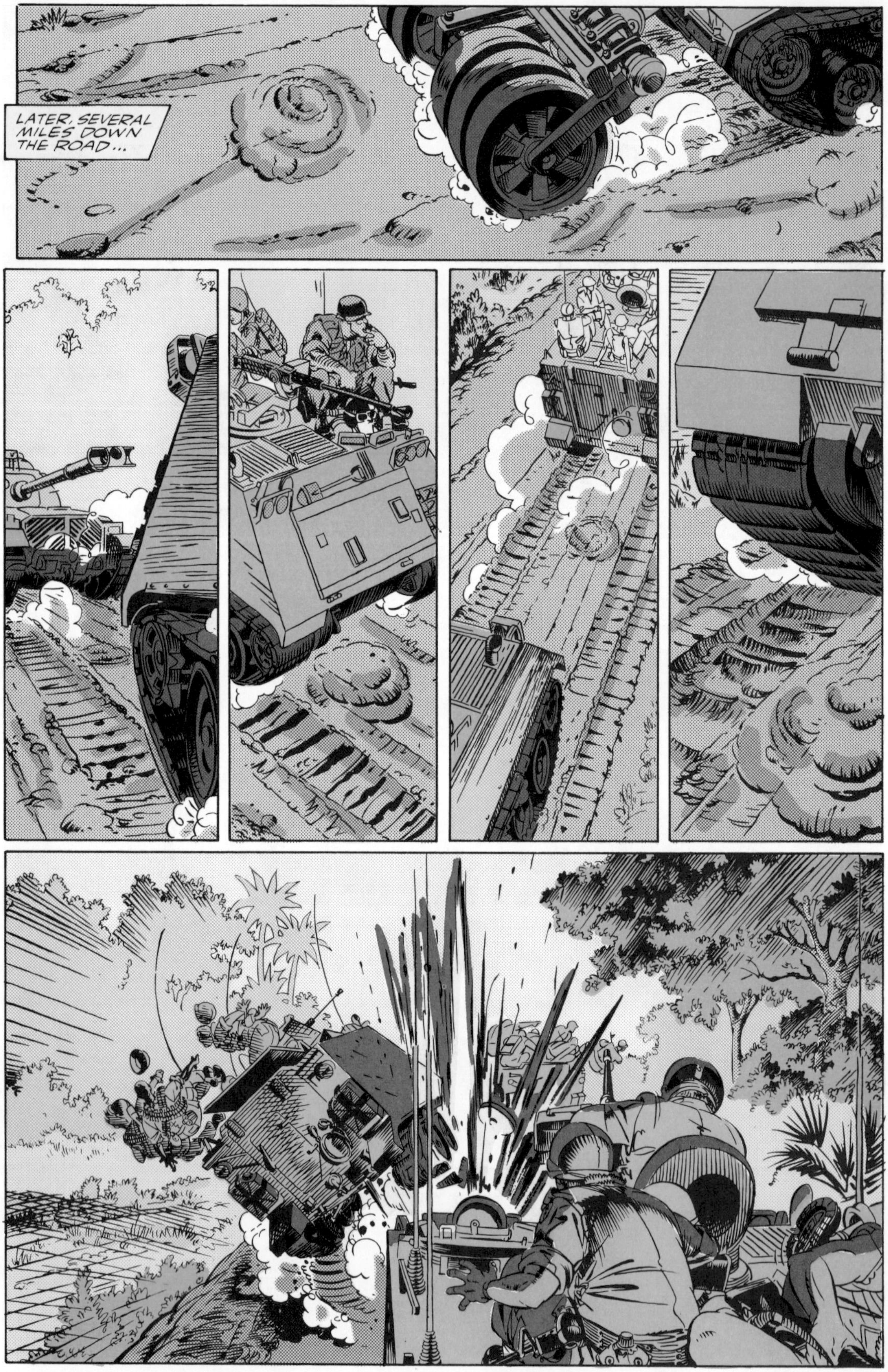
LATER, SEVERAL MILES DOWN THE ROAD...

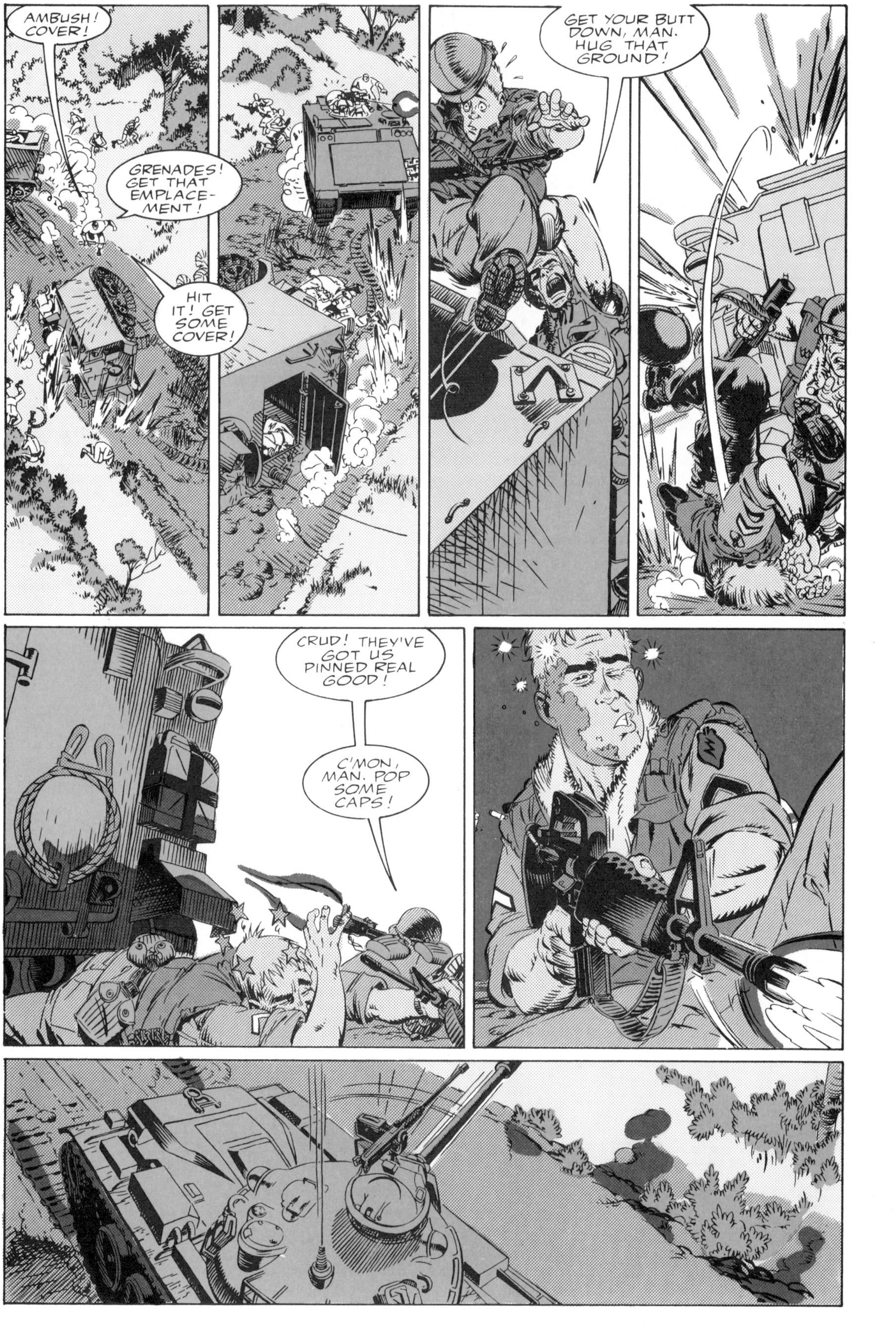
AMBUSH! COVER!
GRENADES! GET THAT EMPLACEMENT!
HIT IT! GET SOME COVER!
GET YOUR BUTT DOWN, MAN. HUG THAT GROUND!
CRUD! THEY'VE GOT US PINNED REAL GOOD!
C'MON, MAN. POP SOME CAPS!

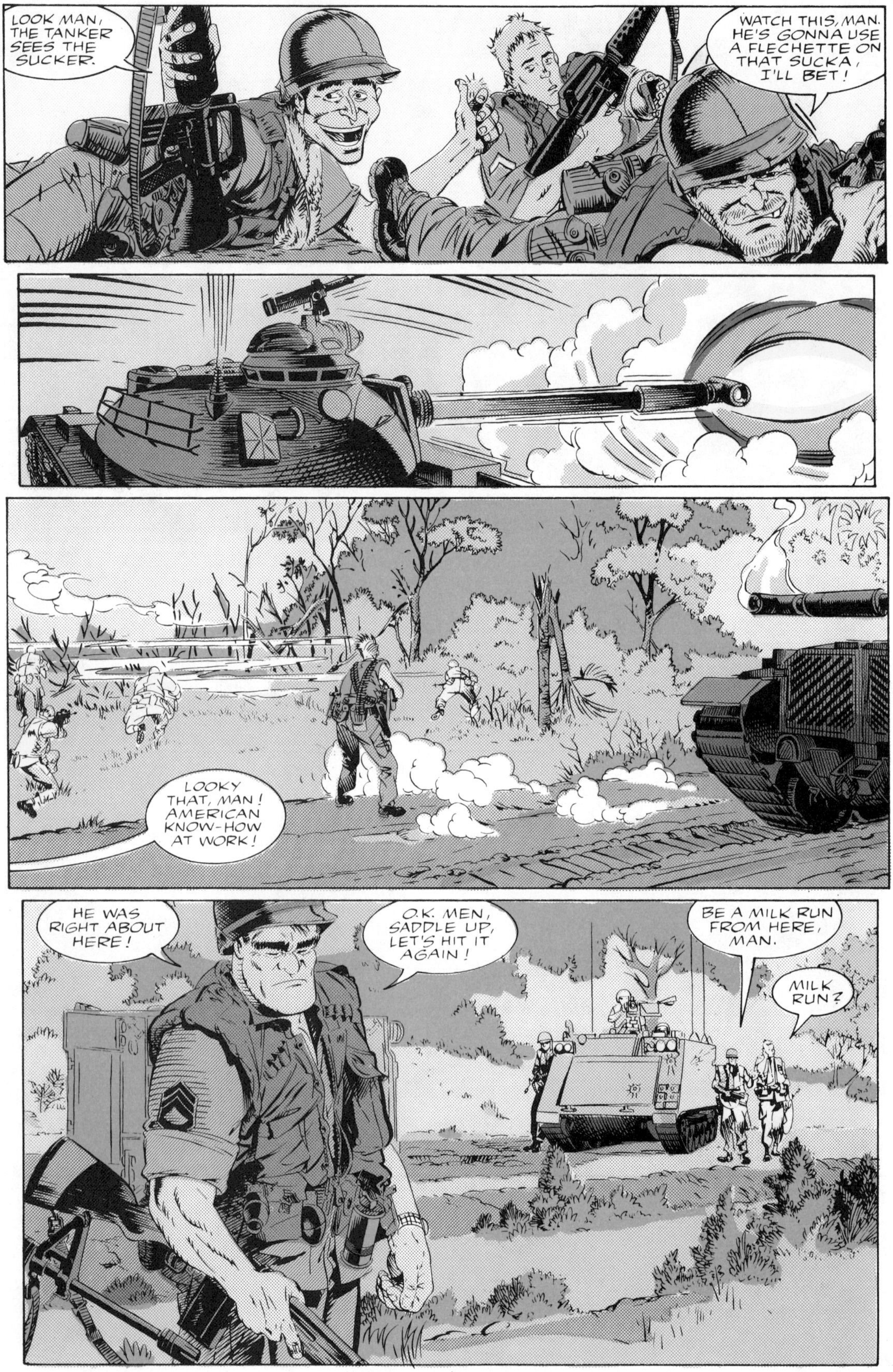
LOOK MAN, THE TANKER SEES THE SUCKER.
WATCH THIS, MAN. HE'S GONNA USE A FLECHETTE ON THAT SUCKA, I'LL BET!
LOOKY THAT, MAN! AMERICAN KNOW-HOW AT WORK!
HE WAS RIGHT ABOUT HERE!
O.K. MEN, SADDLE UP, LET'S HIT IT AGAIN!
BE A MILK RUN FROM HERE, MAN.
MILK RUN?

AND A MILK RUN IT PROVES TO BE.

JEEZ, WHAT A DAY!

DAY, FELT LIKE A WEEK TO ME!

HOME OF
4/23 IN
MECHANIZED OF COURS

DROP THESE IN MY HOOCH FOR ME, WILL'YA, ROG?

SURE THING, SARGE.

THIS TOO, ROG. O.K. MEN, THAT'S IT. HIT THE CLUB. FIRST ROUND'S ON ME!

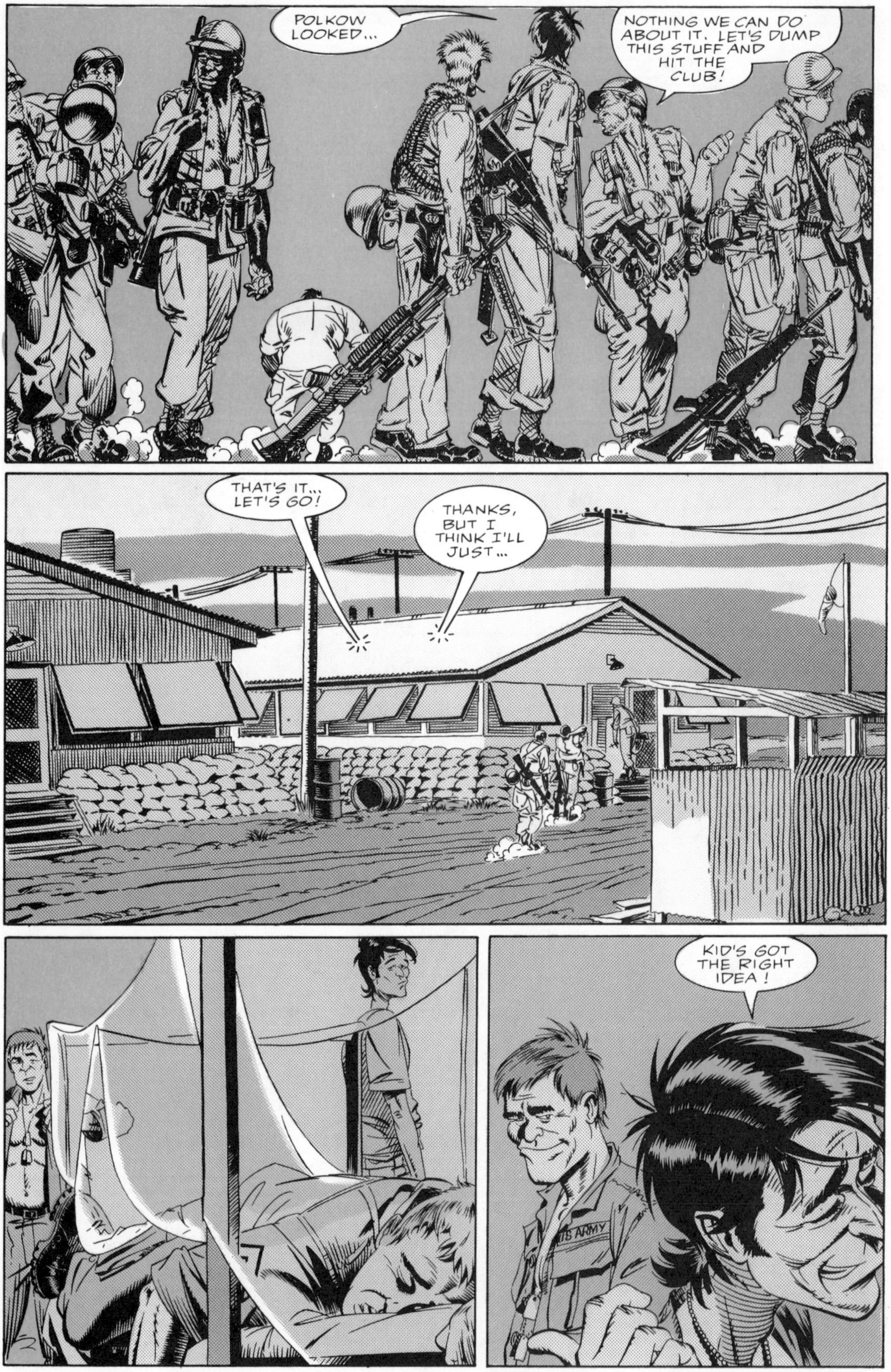
POLKOW LOOKED...
NOTHING WE CAN DO ABOUT IT. LET'S DUMP THIS STUFF AND HIT THE CLUB!
THAT'S IT... LET'S GO!
THANKS, BUT I THINK I'LL JUST...
US ARMY
KID'S GOT THE RIGHT IDEA!

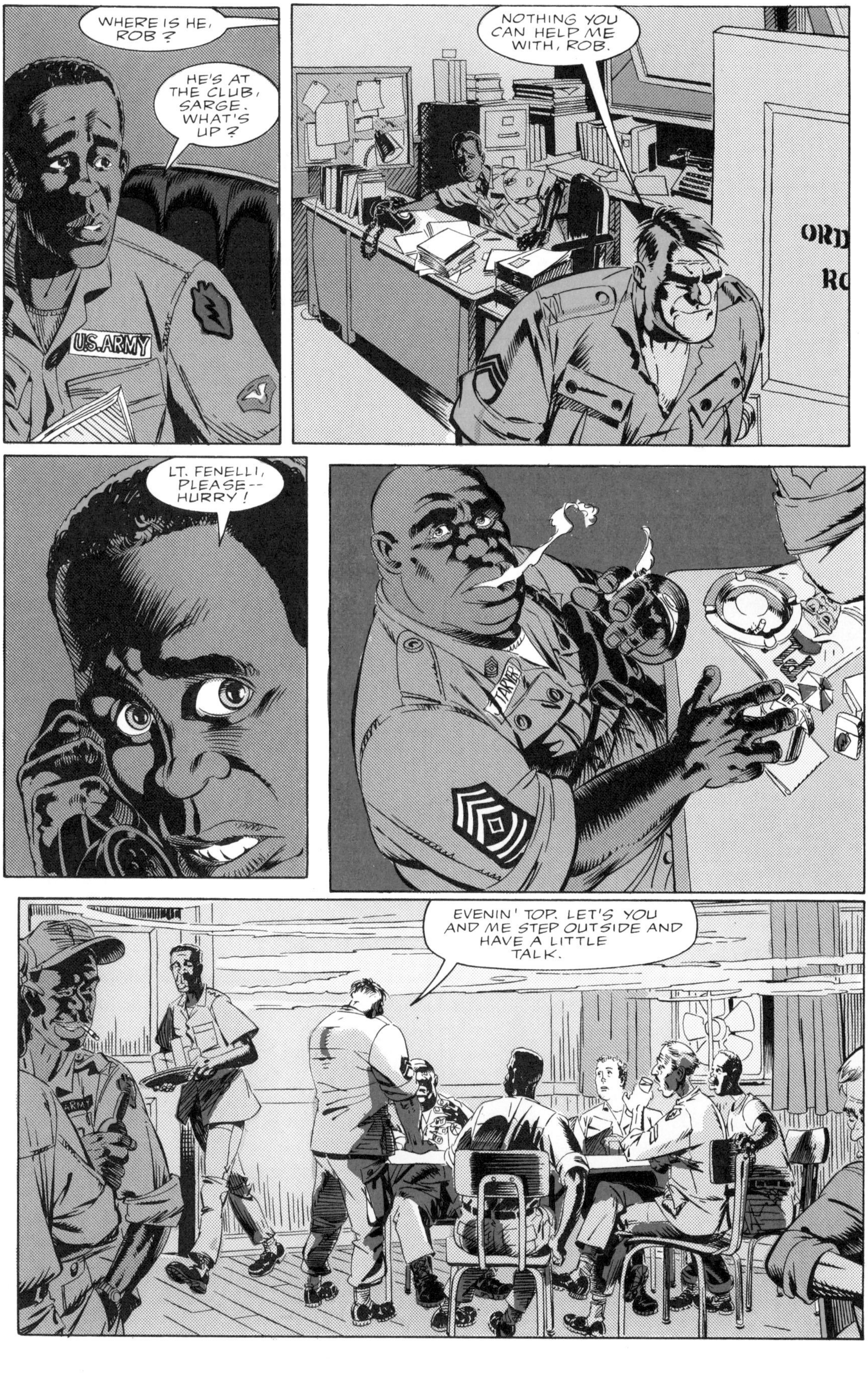
WHERE IS HE, ROB?
HE'S AT THE CLUB, SARGE. WHAT'S UP?
U.S. ARMY
NOTHING YOU CAN HELP ME WITH, ROB.
LT. FENELLI, PLEASE-- HURRY!
EVENIN' TOP. LET'S YOU AND ME STEP OUTSIDE AND HAVE A LITTLE TALK.

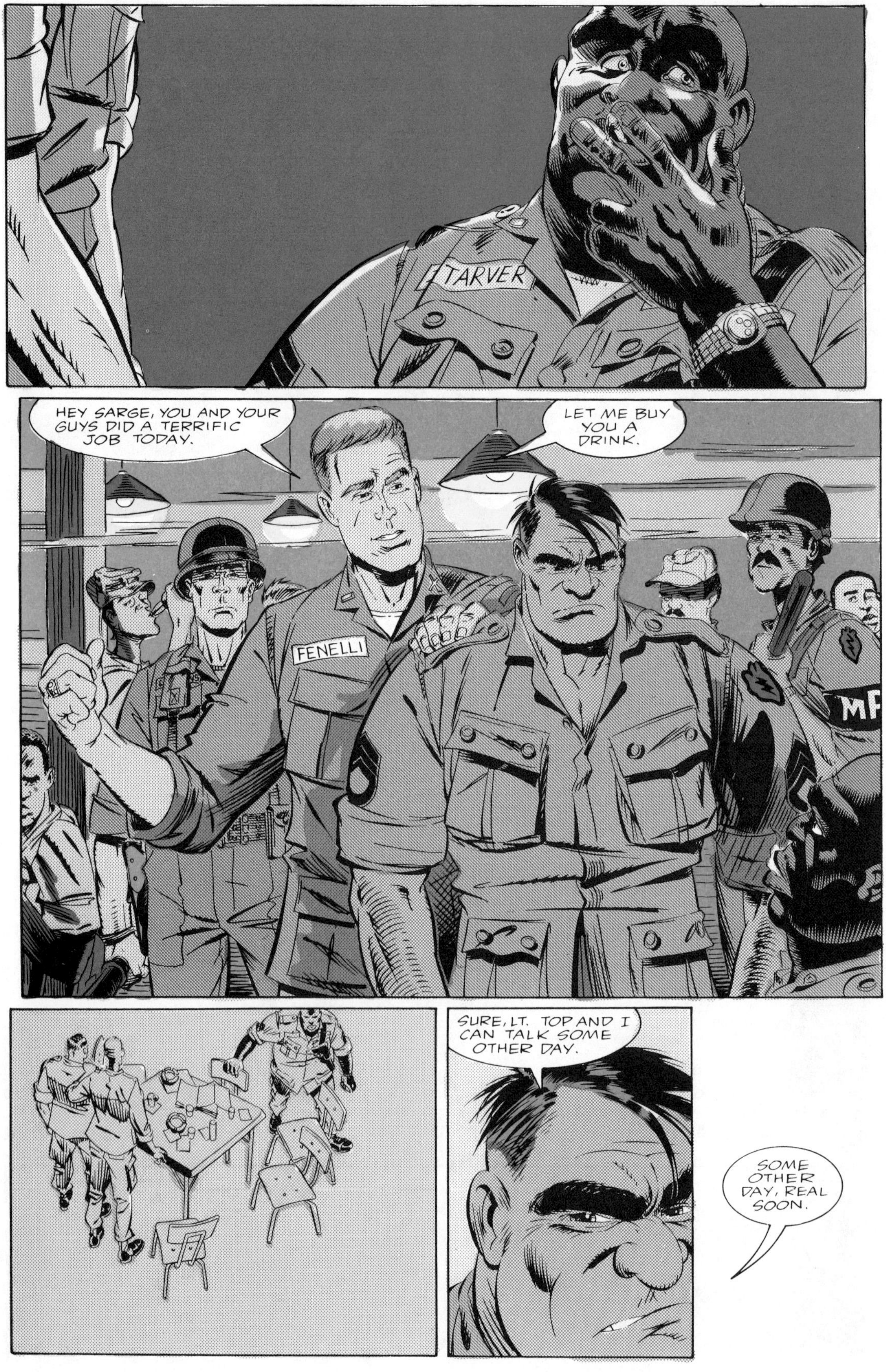
TARVER
HEY SARGE, YOU AND YOUR GUYS DID A TERRIFIC JOB TODAY.
LET ME BUY YOU A DRINK.
FENELLI
MP
SURE, LT. TOP AND I CAN TALK SOME OTHER DAY.
SOME OTHER DAY, REAL SOON.

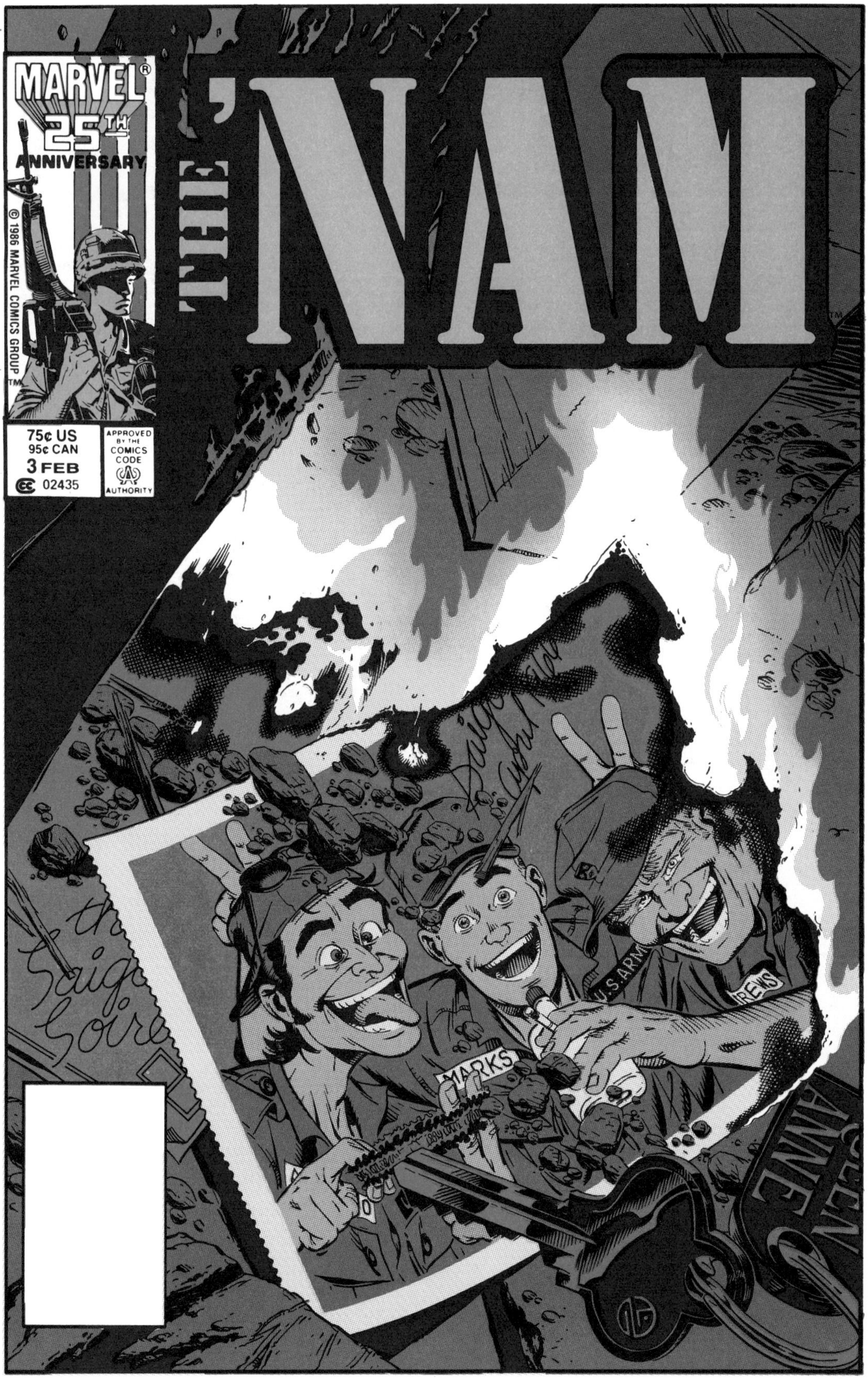
MARVEL
25TH ANNIVERSARY
© 1986 MARVEL COMICS GROUP
THE 'NAM
75¢ US
95¢ CAN
3 FEB
02435
APPROVED BY THE COMICS CODE AUTHORITY
MARKS

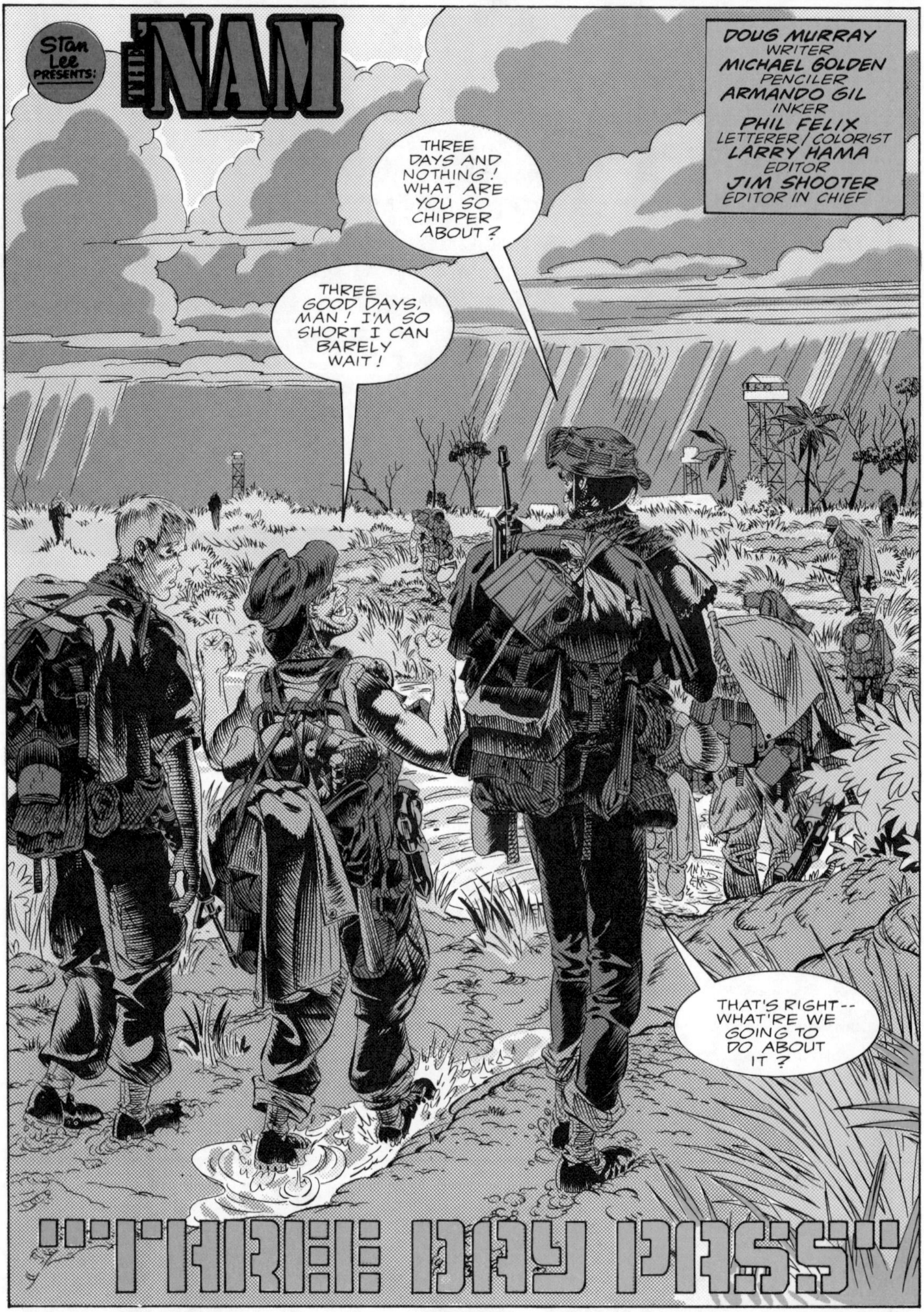
Stan Lee PRESENTS:
THE 'NAM
DOUG MURRAY WRITER
MICHAEL GOLDEN PENCILER
ARMANDO GIL INKER
PHIL FELIX LETTERER / COLORIST
LARRY HAMA EDITOR
JIM SHOOTER EDITOR IN CHIEF
THREE GOOD DAYS, MAN! I'M SO SHORT I CAN BARELY WAIT!
THREE DAYS AND NOTHING! WHAT ARE YOU SO CHIPPER ABOUT?
THAT'S RIGHT-- WHAT'RE WE GOING TO DO ABOUT IT?
"THREE DAY PASS"

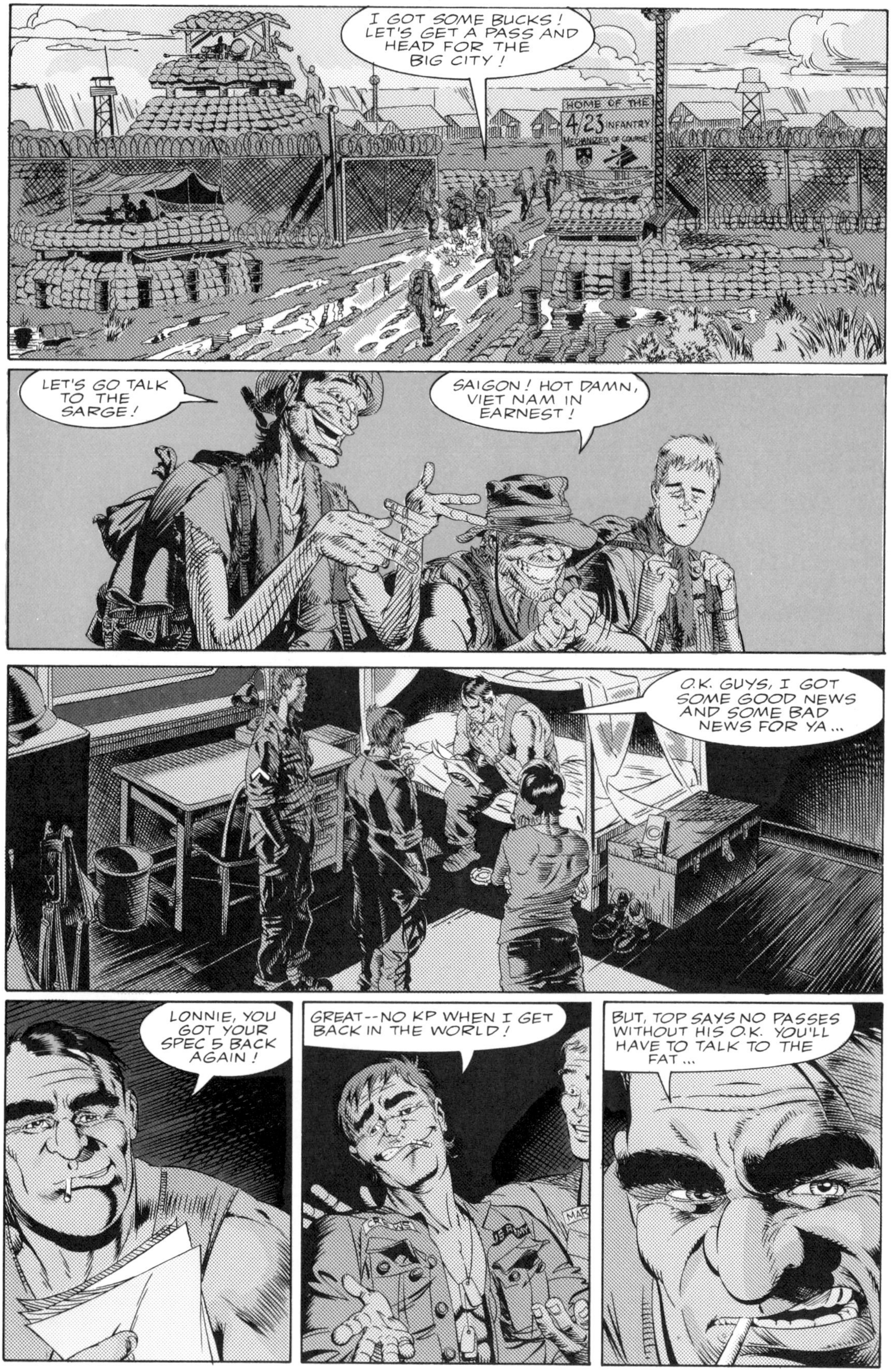
I GOT SOME BUCKS! LET'S GET A PASS AND HEAD FOR THE BIG CITY!
HOME OF THE
4/23 INFANTRY
MECHANIZED OF COURSE!
LET'S GO TALK TO THE SARGE!
SAIGON! HOT DAMN, VIET NAM IN EARNEST!
O.K. GUYS, I GOT SOME GOOD NEWS AND SOME BAD NEWS FOR YA...
LONNIE, YOU GOT YOUR SPEC 5 BACK AGAIN!
GREAT--NO KP WHEN I GET BACK IN THE WORLD!
BUT, TOP SAYS NO PASSES WITHOUT HIS O.K. YOU'LL HAVE TO TALK TO THE FAT...

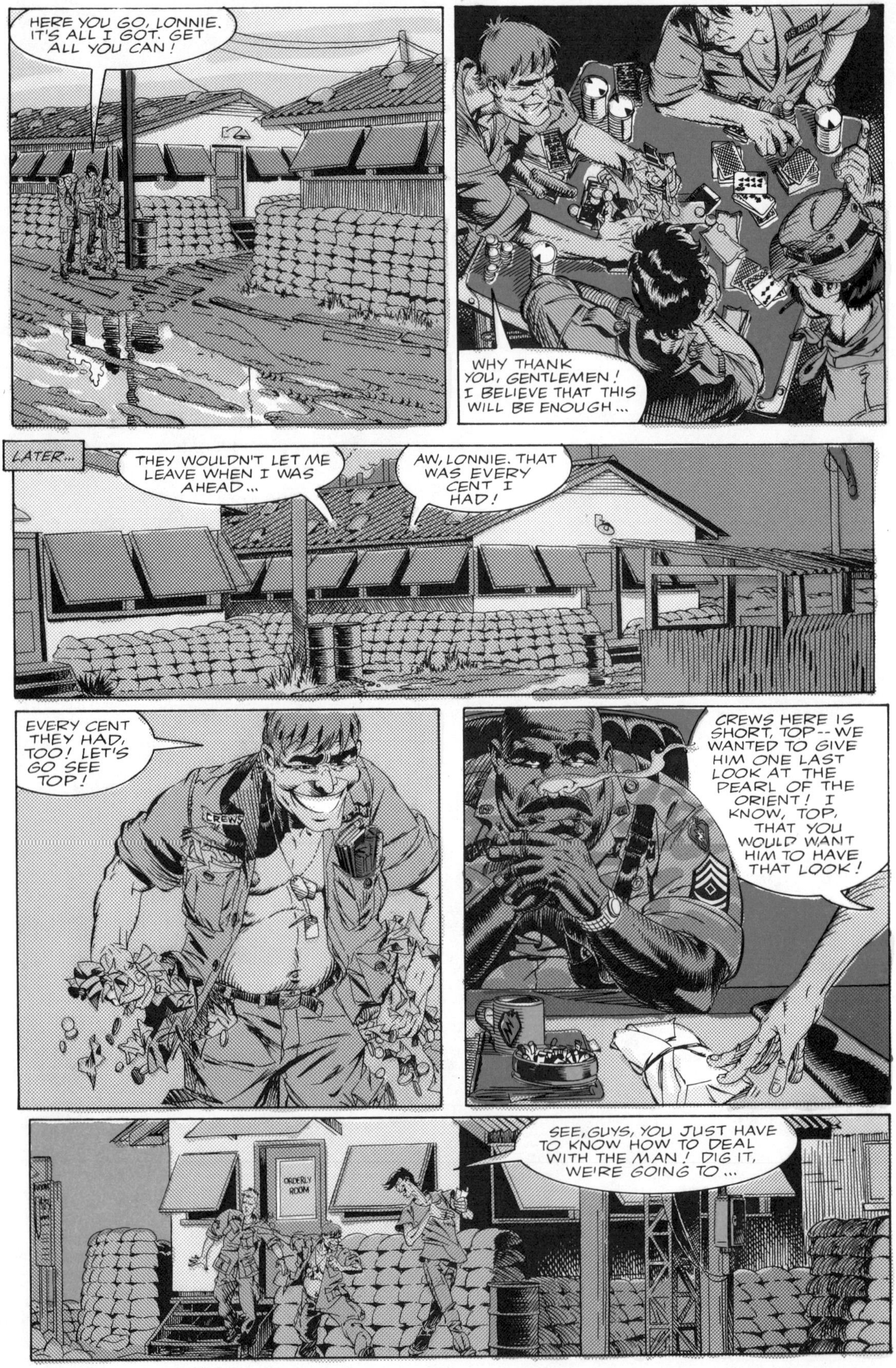
HERE YOU GO, LONNIE. IT'S ALL I GOT. GET ALL YOU CAN!
WHY THANK YOU, GENTLEMEN! I BELIEVE THAT THIS WILL BE ENOUGH...
LATER...
THEY WOULDN'T LET ME LEAVE WHEN I WAS AHEAD...
AW, LONNIE. THAT WAS EVERY CENT I HAD!
EVERY CENT THEY HAD, TOO! LET'S GO SEE TOP!
CREWS
CREWS HERE IS SHORT, TOP-- WE WANTED TO GIVE HIM ONE LAST LOOK AT THE PEARL OF THE ORIENT! I KNOW, TOP, THAT YOU WOULD WANT HIM TO HAVE THAT LOOK!
ORDERLY ROOM
SEE, GUYS, YOU JUST HAVE TO KNOW HOW TO DEAL WITH THE MAN! DIG IT, WE'RE GOING TO...

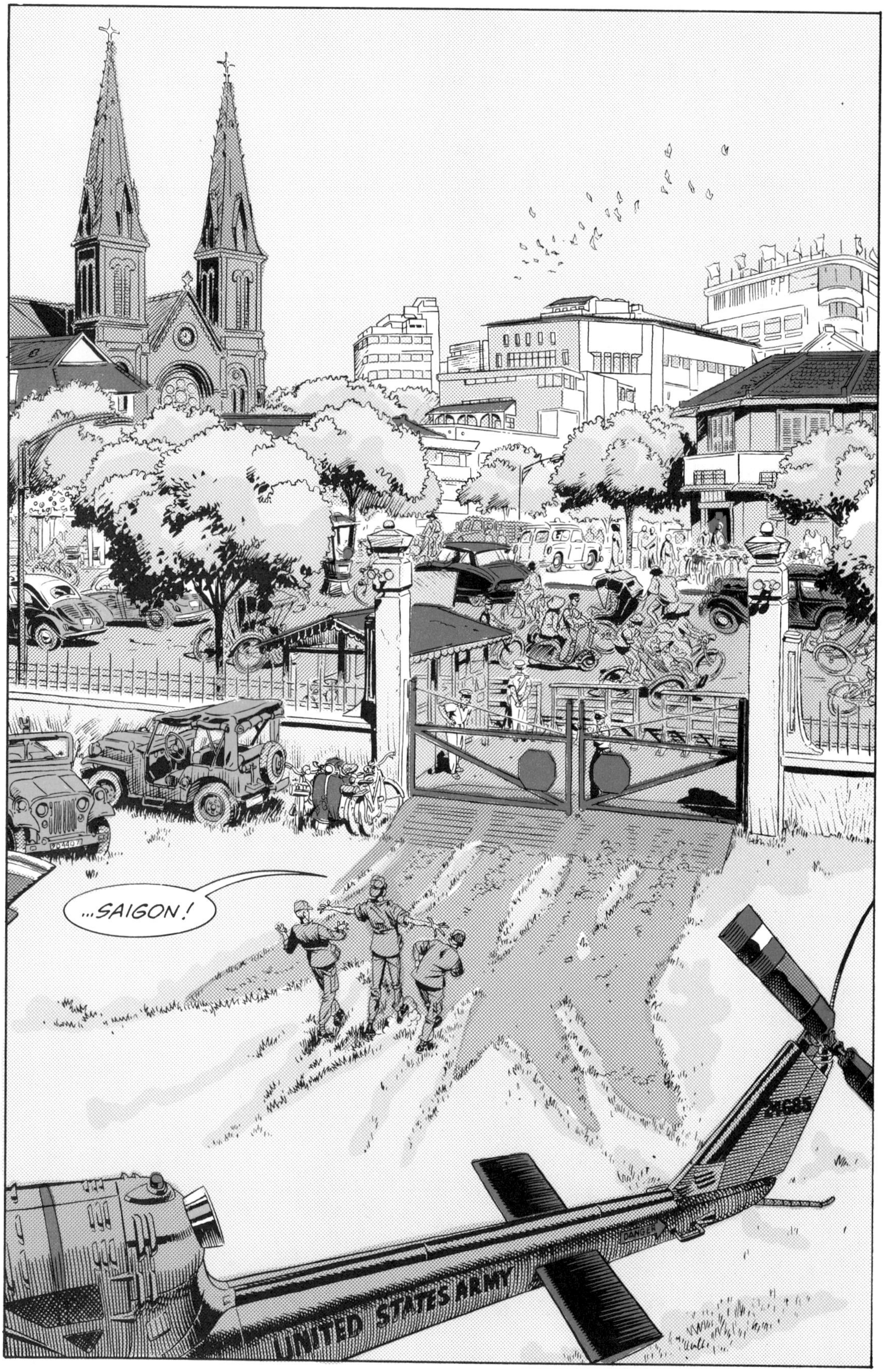
...SAIGON!
DANGER
UNITED STATES ARMY

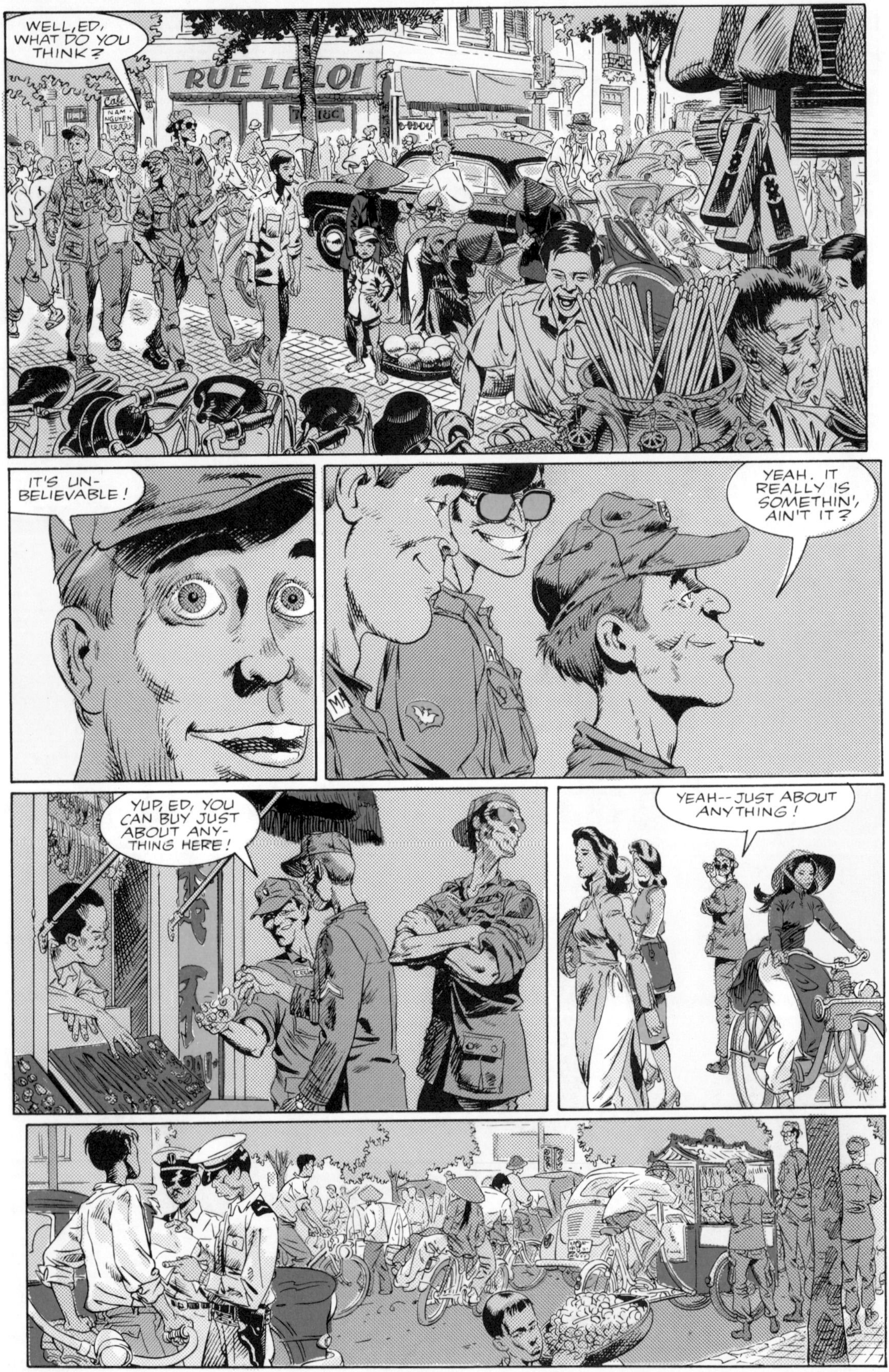
WELL, ED, WHAT DO YOU THINK?
RUE LELOI
IT'S UN-BELIEVABLE!
YEAH. IT REALLY IS SOMETHIN', AIN'T IT?
YUP, ED, YOU CAN BUY JUST ABOUT ANY-THING HERE!
YEAH--JUST ABOUT ANYTHING!

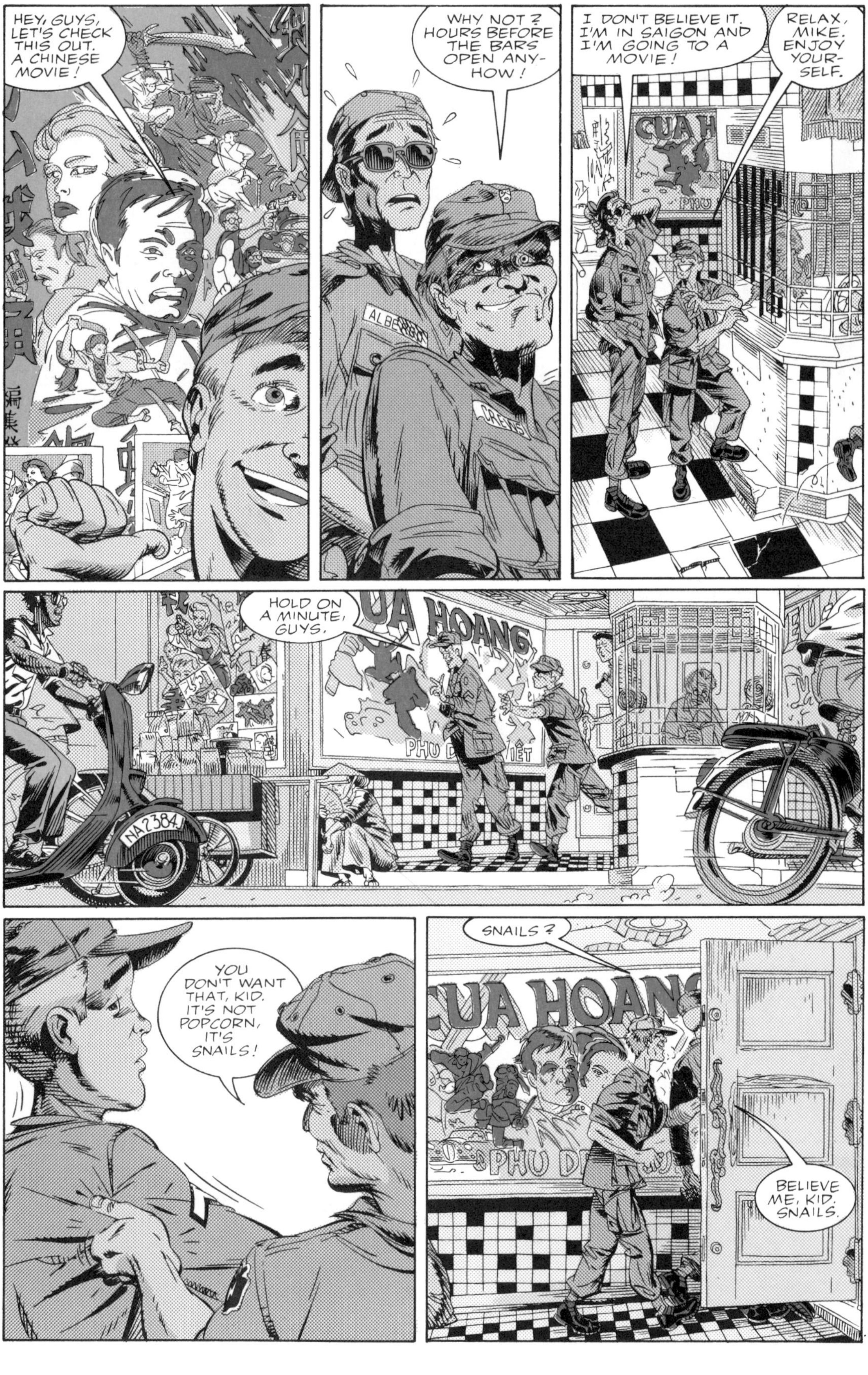
HEY, GUYS, LET'S CHECK THIS OUT. A CHINESE MOVIE!
WHY NOT? HOURS BEFORE THE BARS OPEN ANY-HOW!
I DON'T BELIEVE IT. I'M IN SAIGON AND I'M GOING TO A MOVIE!
RELAX, MIKE. ENJOY YOUR-SELF.
HOLD ON A MINUTE, GUYS.
CUA HOANG
NA2384
YOU DON'T WANT THAT, KID. IT'S NOT POPCORN, IT'S SNAILS!
SNAILS?
BELIEVE ME, KID. SNAILS.

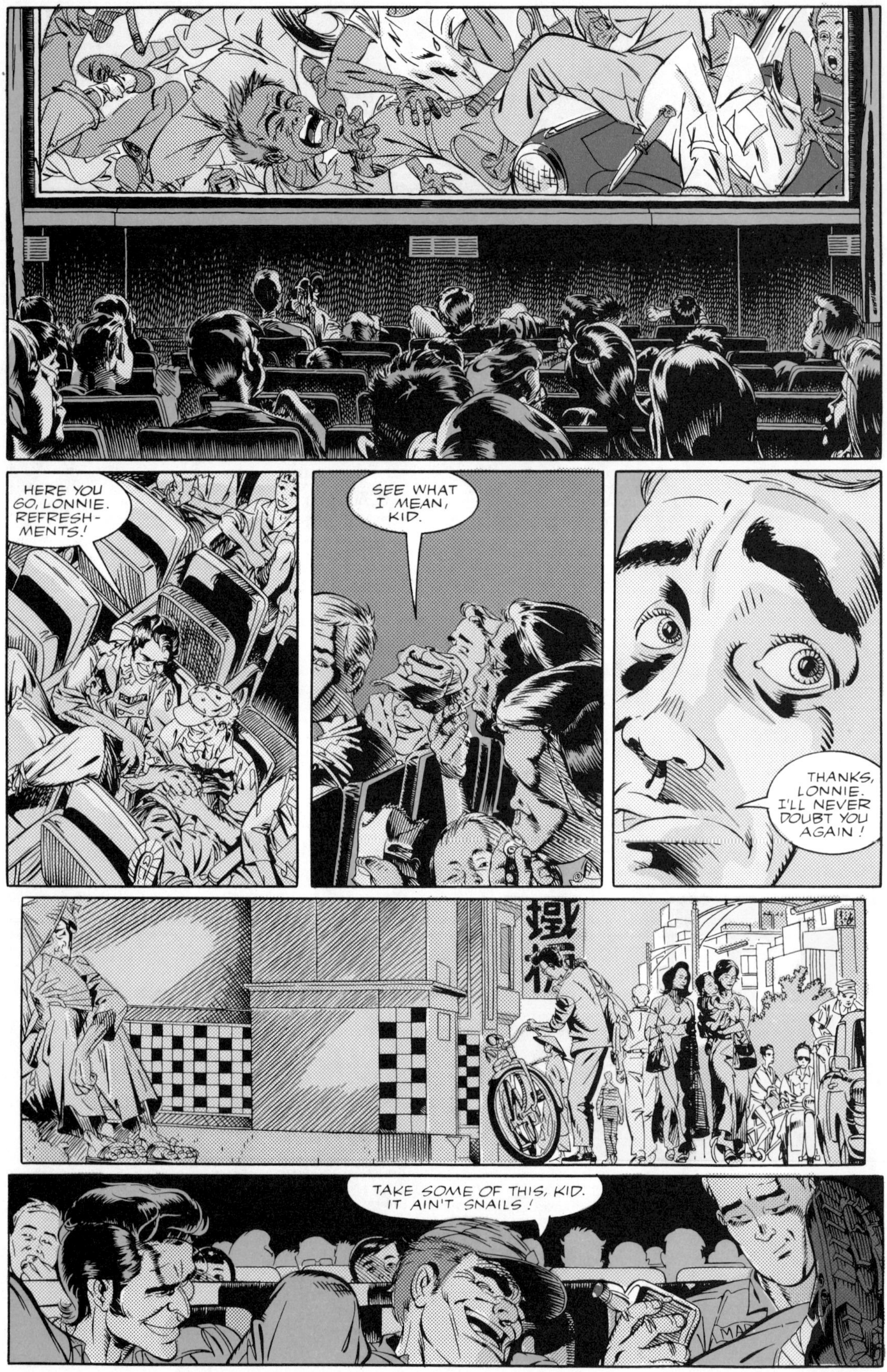
HERE YOU GO, LONNIE. REFRESH-MENTS!
SEE WHAT I MEAN, KID.
THANKS, LONNIE. I'LL NEVER DOUBT YOU AGAIN!
TAKE SOME OF THIS, KID. IT AIN'T SNAILS!

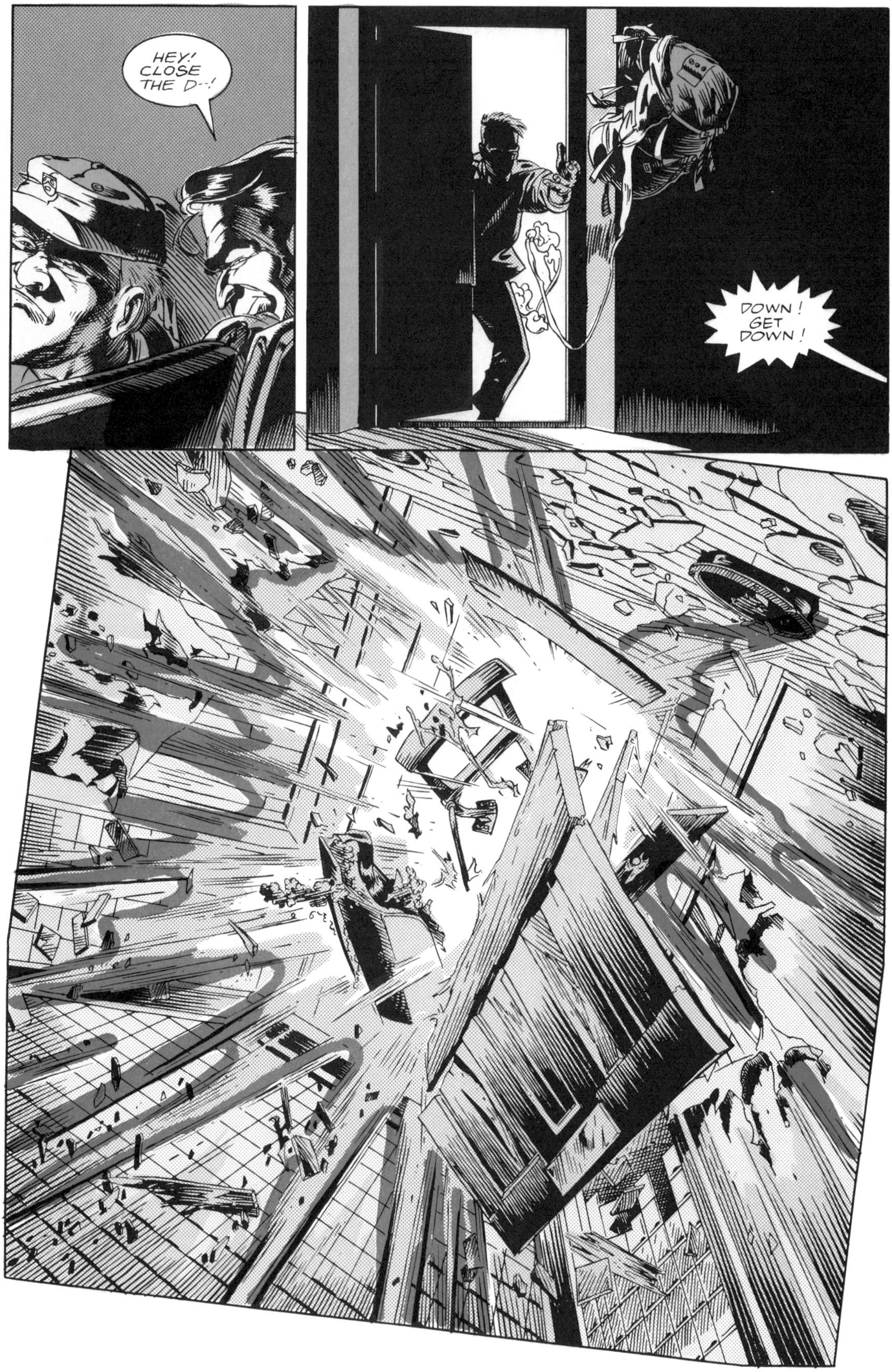
HEY! CLOSE THE D--!
DOWN! GET DOWN!

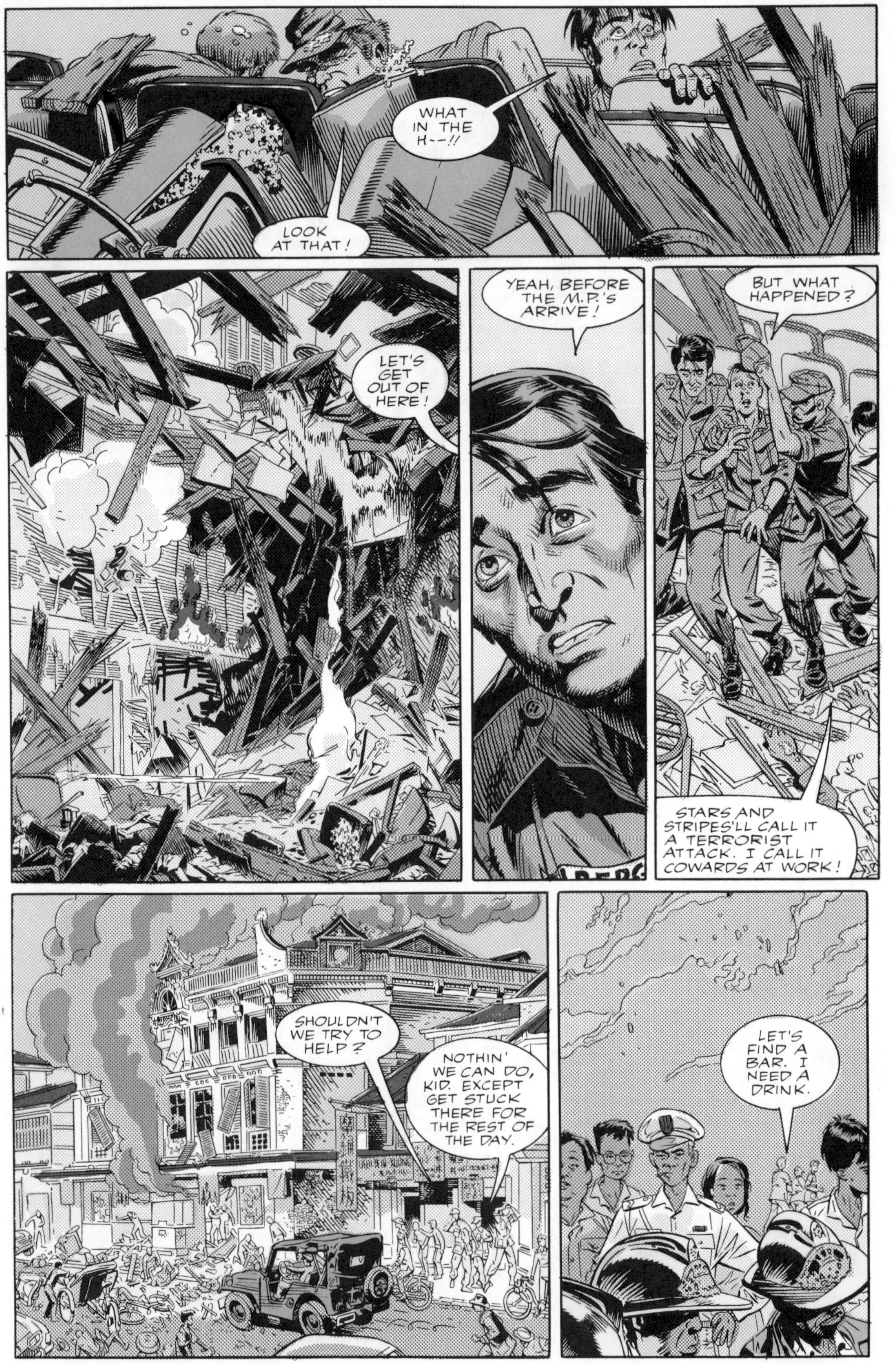
WHAT IN THE H--!!
LOOK AT THAT!
LET'S GET OUT OF HERE!
YEAH, BEFORE THE M.P.'s ARRIVE!
BUT WHAT HAPPENED?
STARS AND STRIPES'LL CALL IT A TERRORIST ATTACK. I CALL IT COWARDS AT WORK!
SHOULDN'T WE TRY TO HELP?
NOTHIN' WE CAN DO, KID. EXCEPT GET STUCK THERE FOR THE REST OF THE DAY.
LET'S FIND A BAR. I NEED A DRINK.

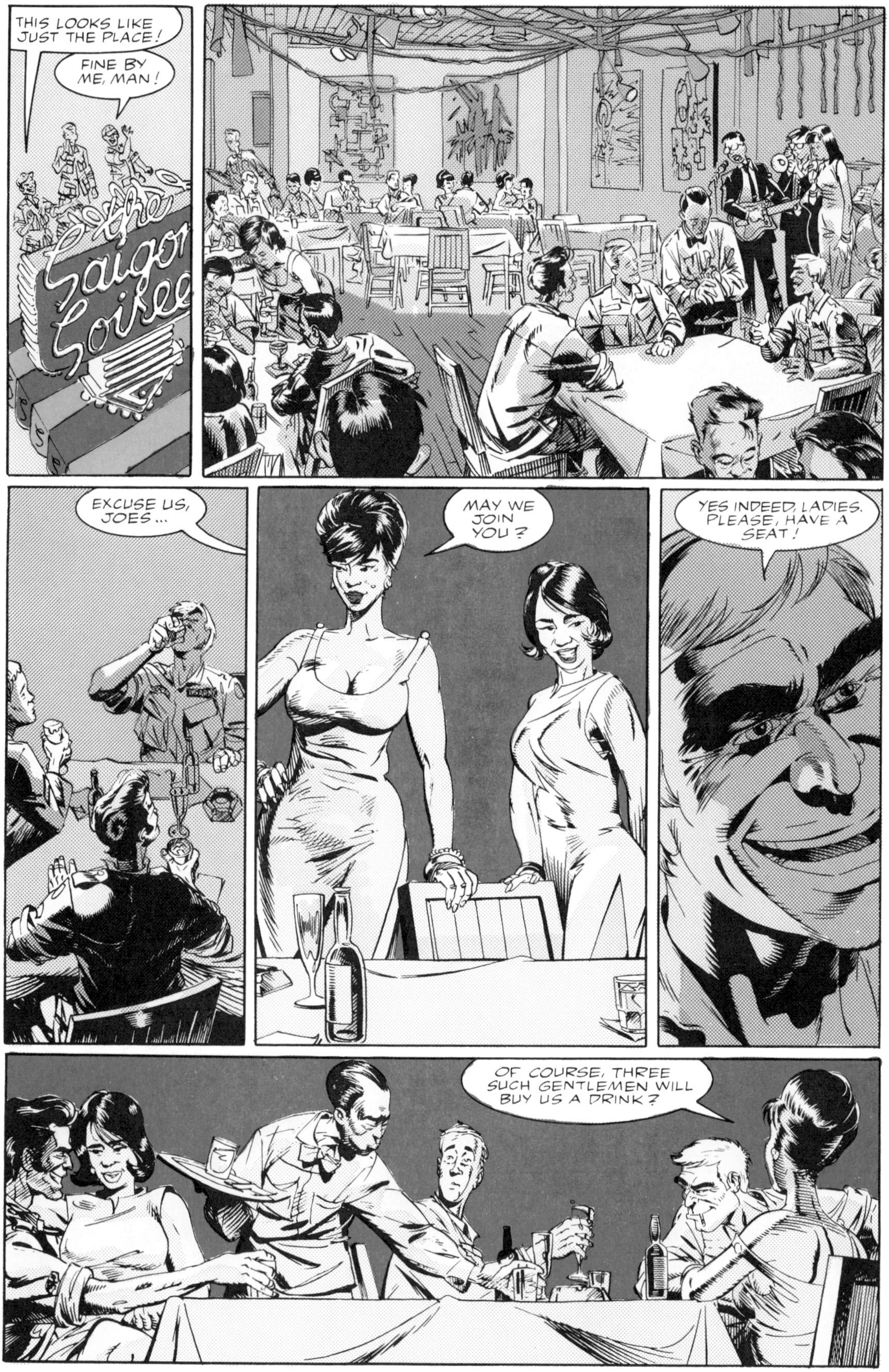
THIS LOOKS LIKE JUST THE PLACE!
FINE BY ME, MAN!
the Saigon Soiree
EXCUSE US, JOES...
MAY WE JOIN YOU?
YES INDEED, LADIES. PLEASE, HAVE A SEAT!
OF COURSE, THREE SUCH GENTLEMEN WILL BUY US A DRINK?

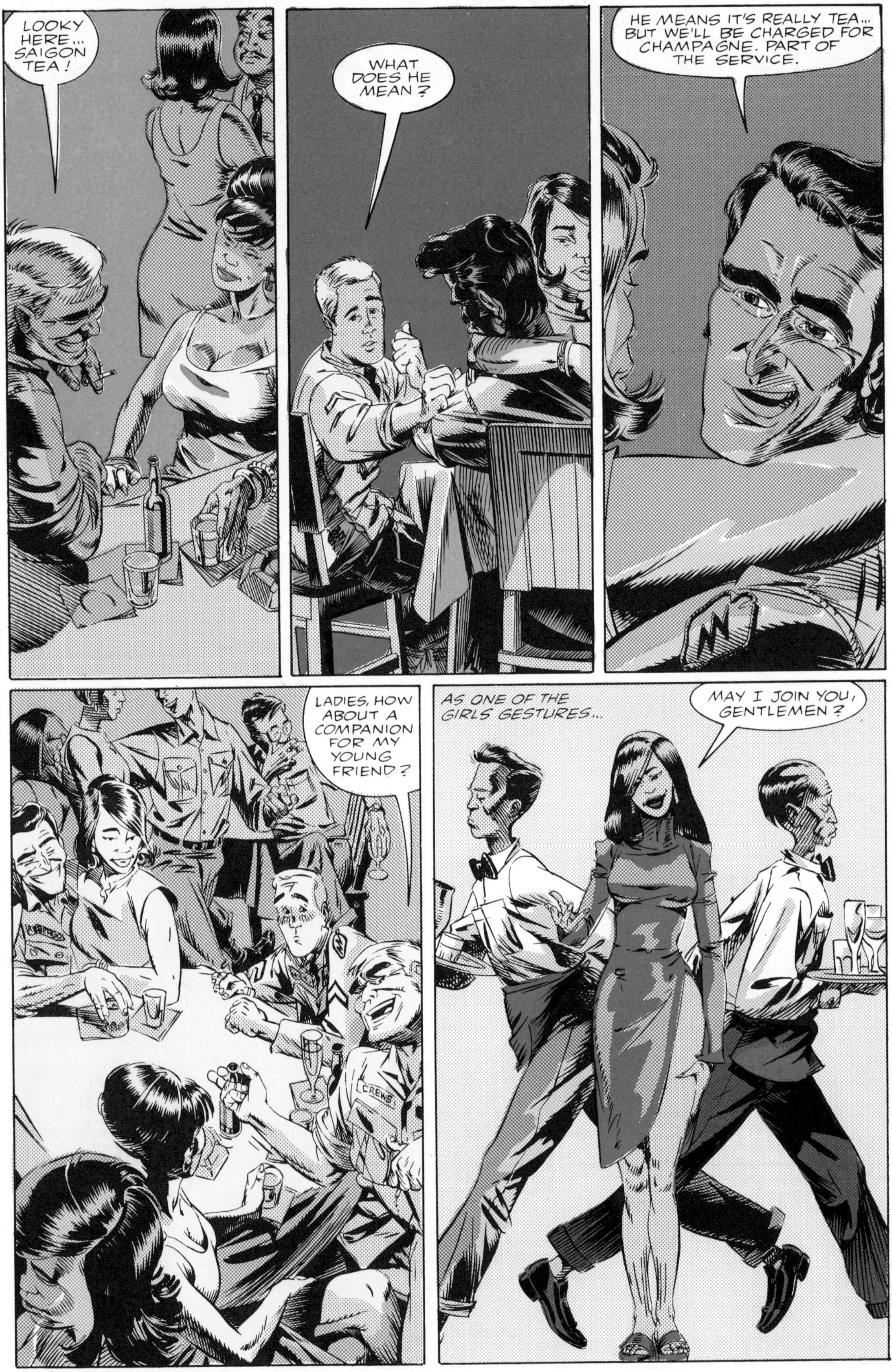
LOOKY HERE... SAIGON TEA!
WHAT DOES HE MEAN?
HE MEANS IT'S REALLY TEA... BUT WE'LL BE CHARGED FOR CHAMPAGNE. PART OF THE SERVICE.
LADIES, HOW ABOUT A COMPANION FOR MY YOUNG FRIEND?
CREWS
AS ONE OF THE GIRLS GESTURES...
MAY I JOIN YOU, GENTLEMEN?

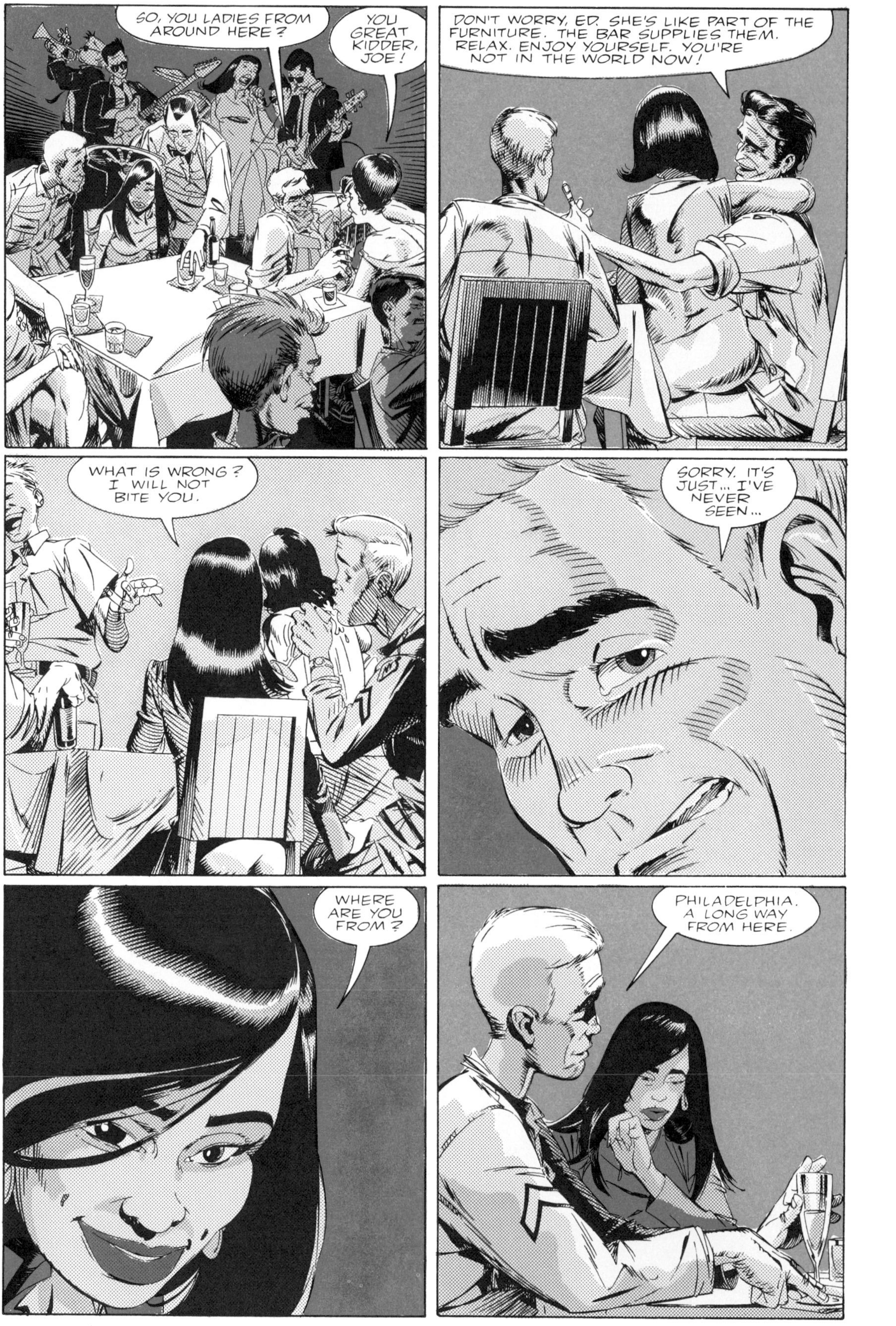
SO, YOU LADIES FROM AROUND HERE ?
YOU GREAT KIDDER, JOE !
DON'T WORRY, ED. SHE'S LIKE PART OF THE FURNITURE. THE BAR SUPPLIES THEM. RELAX. ENJOY YOURSELF. YOU'RE NOT IN THE WORLD NOW !
WHAT IS WRONG ? I WILL NOT BITE YOU.
SORRY. IT'S JUST... I'VE NEVER SEEN...
WHERE ARE YOU FROM ?
PHILADELPHIA. A LONG WAY FROM HERE.

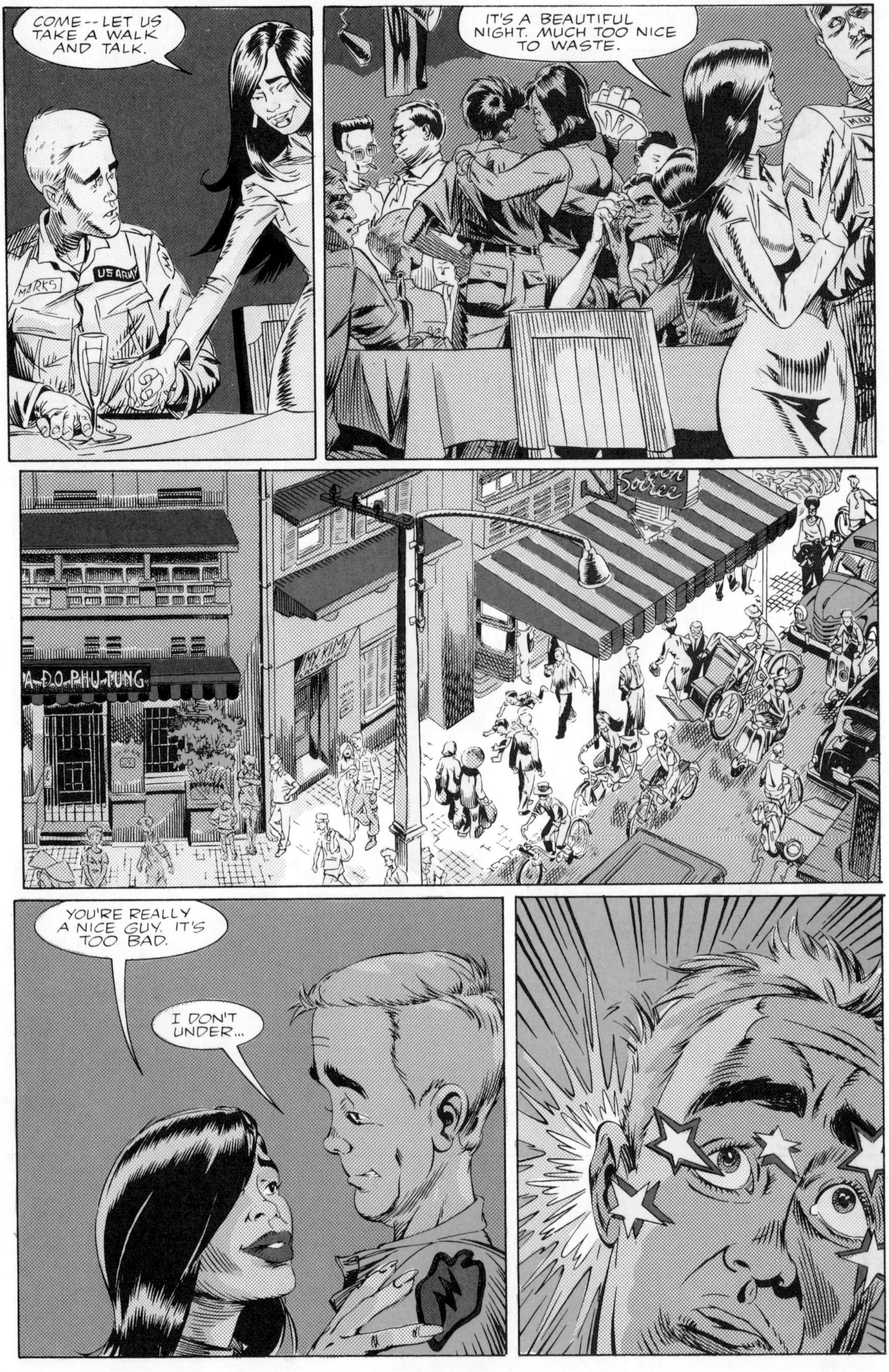
COME--LET US TAKE A WALK AND TALK.
MARKS
US ARMY
IT'S A BEAUTIFUL NIGHT. MUCH TOO NICE TO WASTE.
A DO PHU TUNG
YOU'RE REALLY A NICE GUY. IT'S TOO BAD.
I DON'T UNDER...

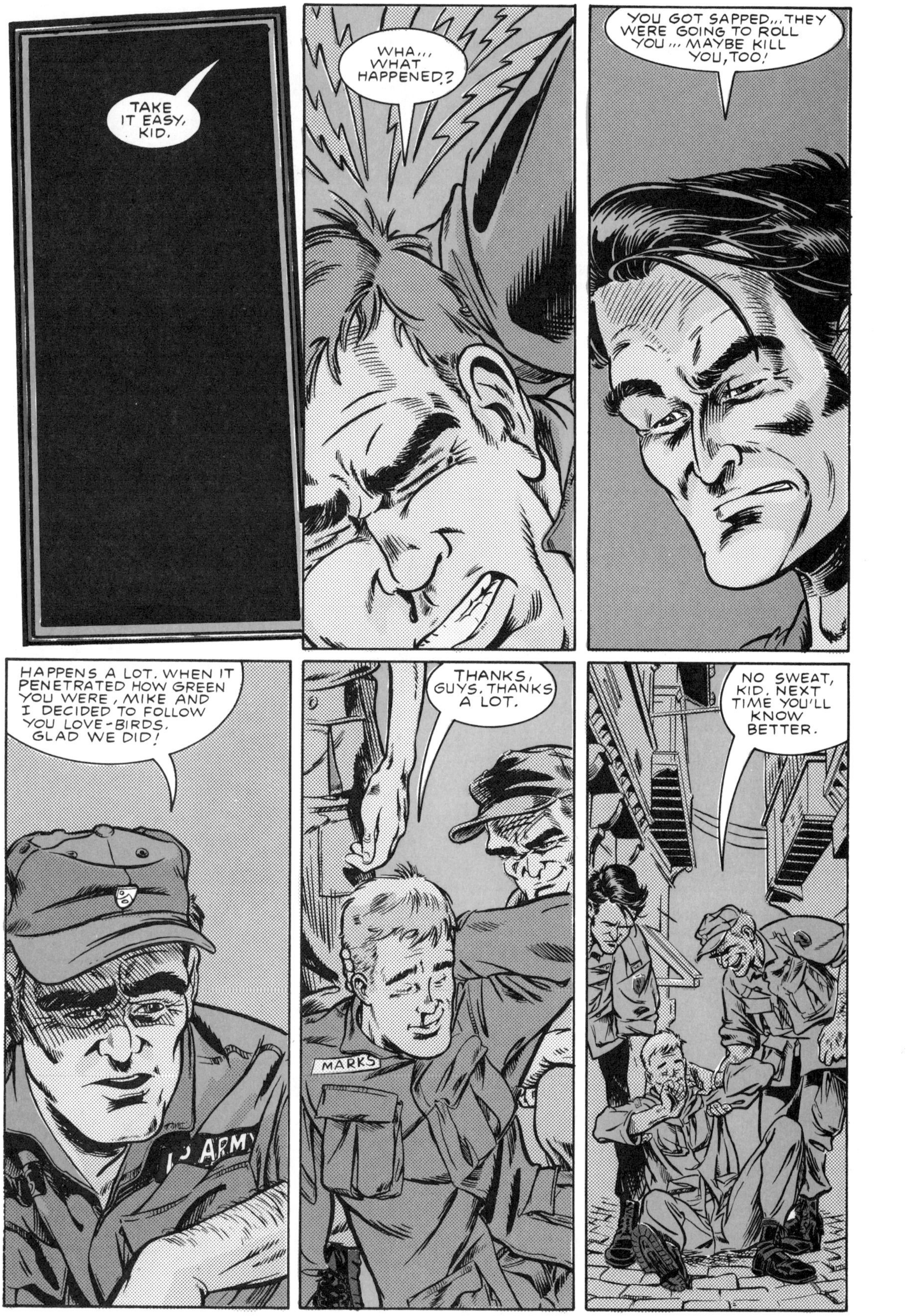
TAKE IT EASY, KID.
WHA... WHAT HAPPENED?
YOU GOT SAPPED... THEY WERE GOING TO ROLL YOU... MAYBE KILL YOU, TOO!
HAPPENS A LOT. WHEN IT PENETRATED HOW GREEN YOU WERE, MIKE AND I DECIDED TO FOLLOW YOU LOVE-BIRDS. GLAD WE DID!
THANKS, GUYS. THANKS A LOT.
MARKS
NO SWEAT, KID. NEXT TIME YOU'LL KNOW BETTER.

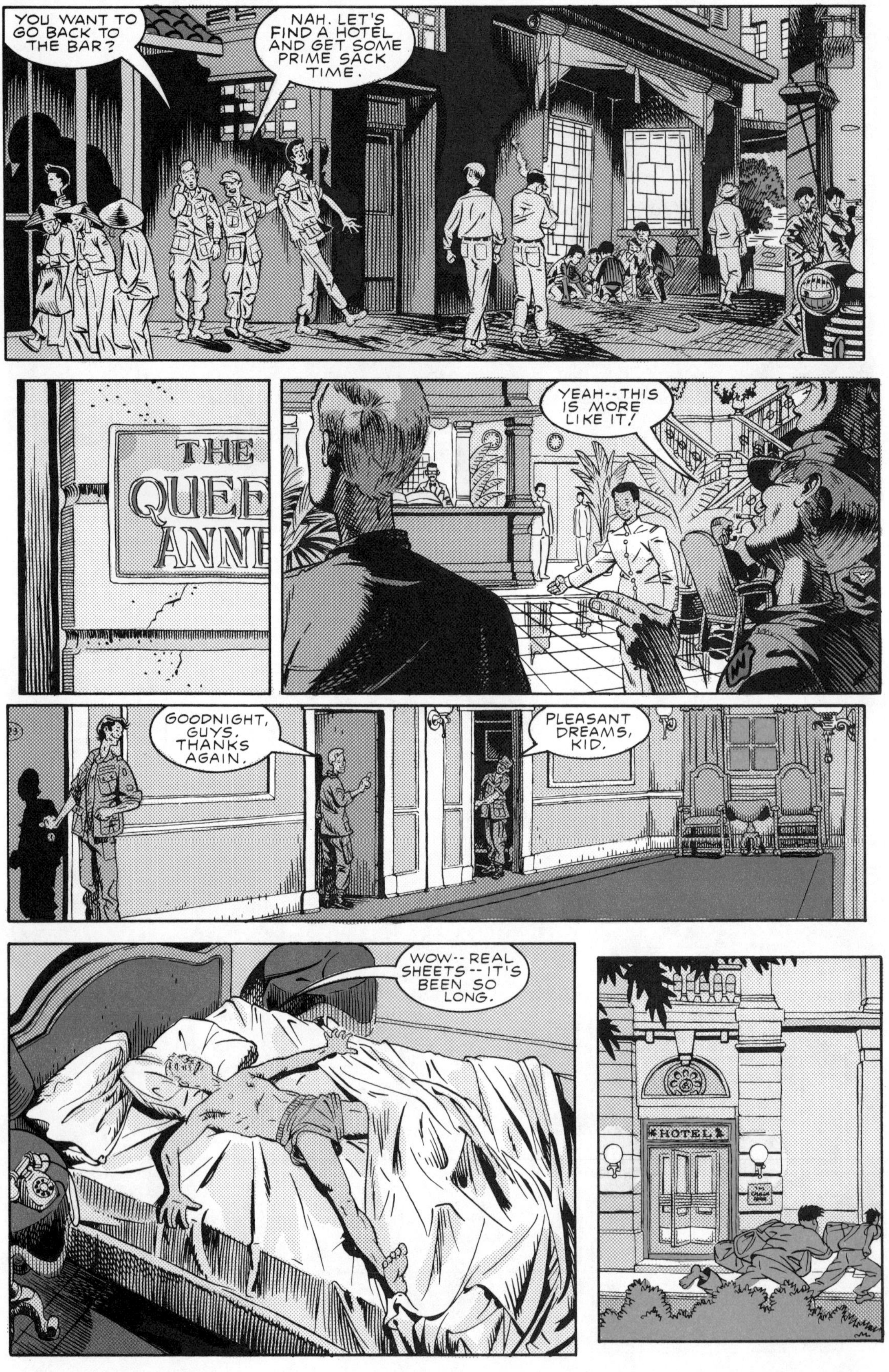
YOU WANT TO GO BACK TO THE BAR?
NAH. LET'S FIND A HOTEL AND GET SOME PRIME SACK TIME.
THE QUEE ANNE
YEAH--THIS IS MORE LIKE IT!
GOODNIGHT, GUYS. THANKS AGAIN.
PLEASANT DREAMS, KID.
WOW--REAL SHEETS--IT'S BEEN SO LONG.
HOTEL

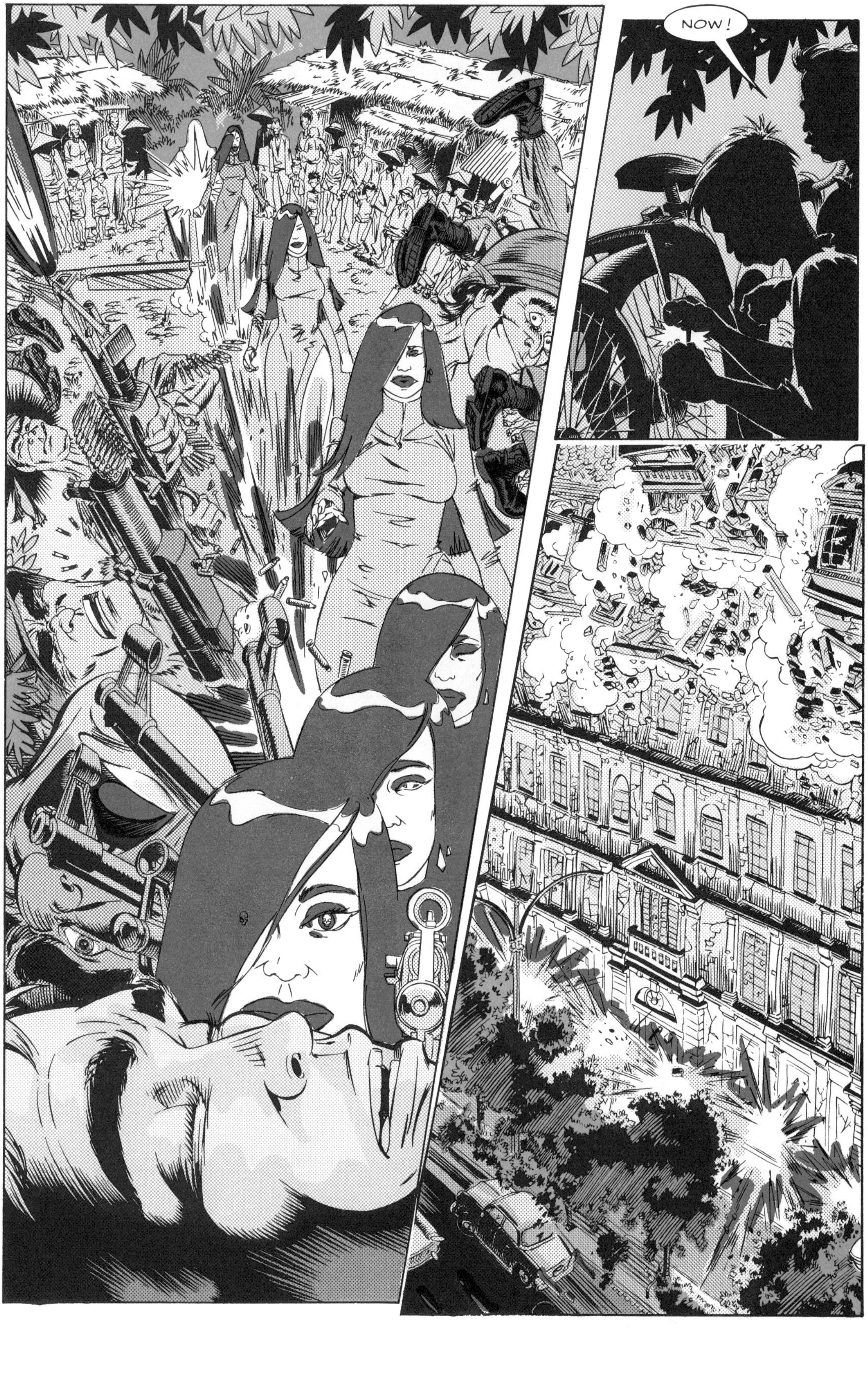
NOW!

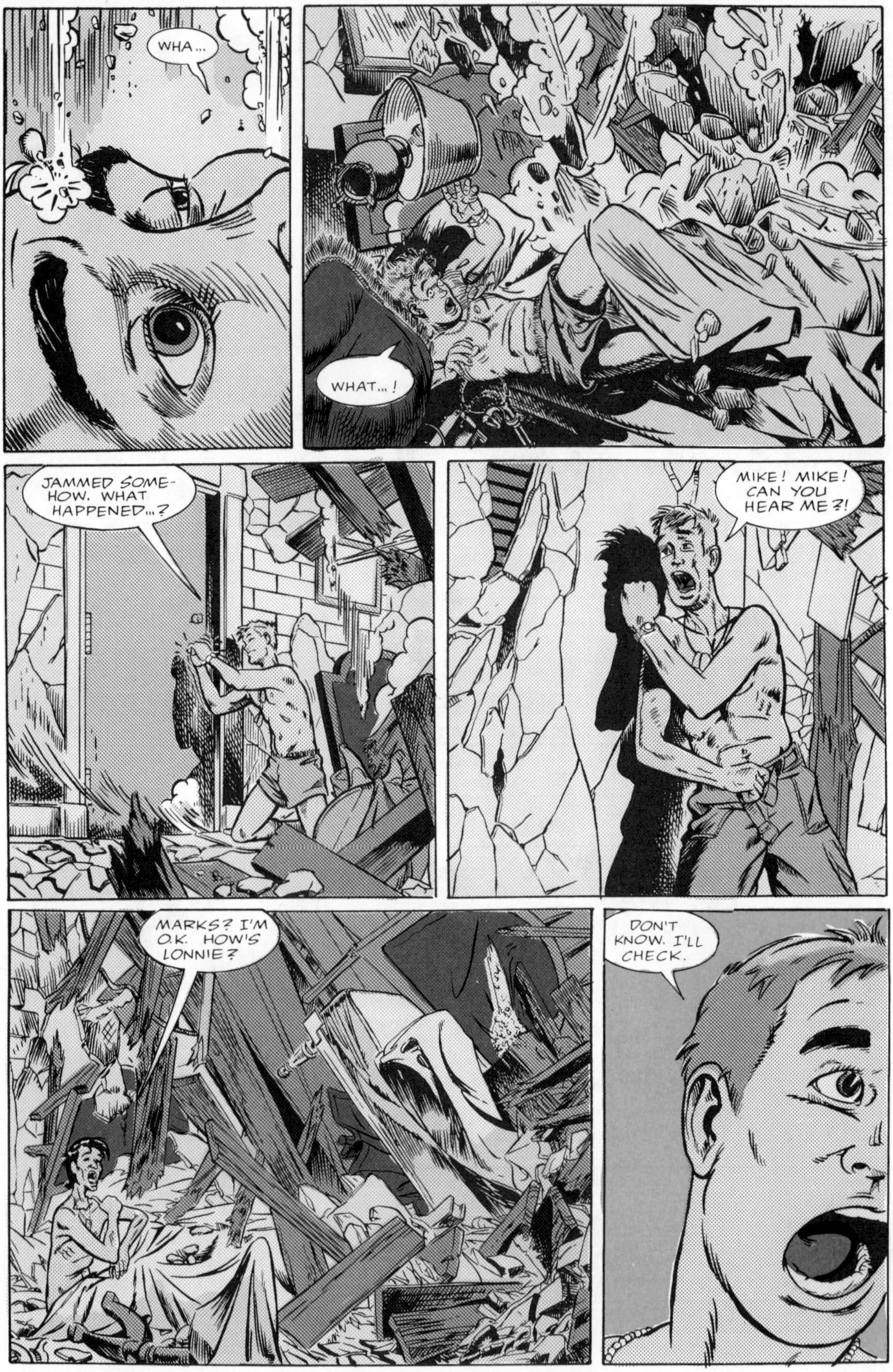
WHA...
WHAT...!
JAMMED SOME-HOW. WHAT HAPPENED...?
MIKE! MIKE! CAN YOU HEAR ME?!
MARKS? I'M O.K. HOW'S LONNIE?
DON'T KNOW. I'LL CHECK.

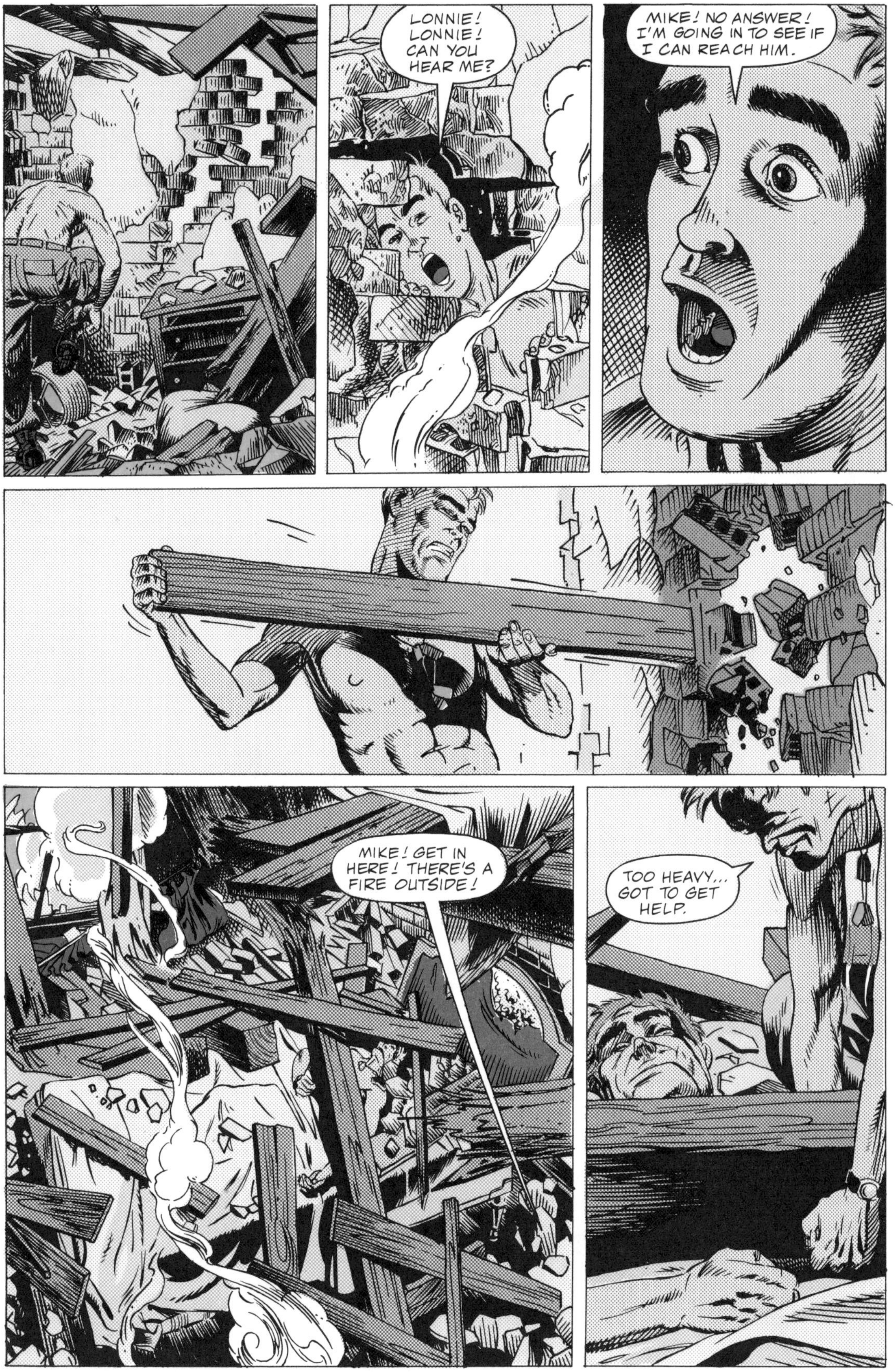
LONNIE! LONNIE! CAN YOU HEAR ME?
MIKE! NO ANSWER! I'M GOING IN TO SEE IF I CAN REACH HIM.
MIKE! GET IN HERE! THERE'S A FIRE OUTSIDE!
TOO HEAVY... GOT TO GET HELP.

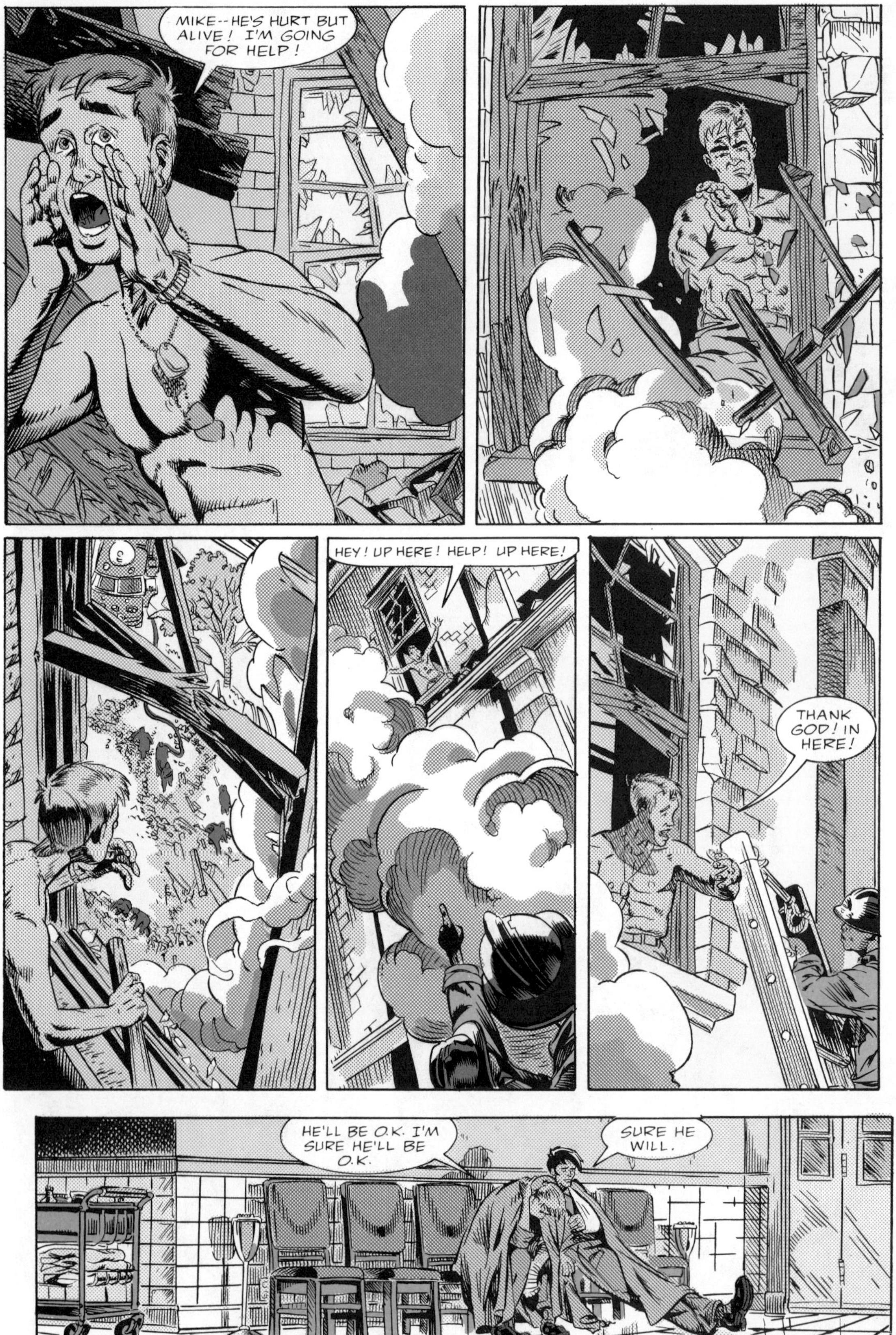
MIKE--HE'S HURT BUT ALIVE! I'M GOING FOR HELP!
HEY! UP HERE! HELP! UP HERE!
THANK GOD! IN HERE!
HE'LL BE O.K. I'M SURE HE'LL BE O.K.
SURE HE WILL.

LATER...

JUST A FEW MINUTES, MEN!

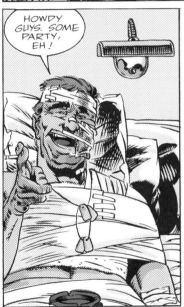

HOWDY GUYS. SOME PARTY, EH!

YOU OKAY, LONNIE?

OH, YEAH. JUST A COUPLA BROKEN RIBS. DOC SAYS, BEIN' AS I'M SHORT, THEY'LL JUST HOLD ME HERE AND SHIP ME OUT IN A FEW DAYS. HEY MAN, I'M GOIN' BACK TO THE WORLD!

AND YOU GUYS SAW THE HIRED HELP!

YEAH, I SEE WHAT YOU MEAN, YOU OLD REPROBATE!

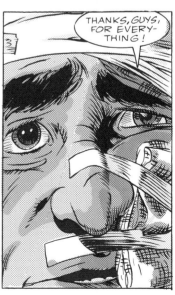

THANKS, GUYS, FOR EVERY-THING!

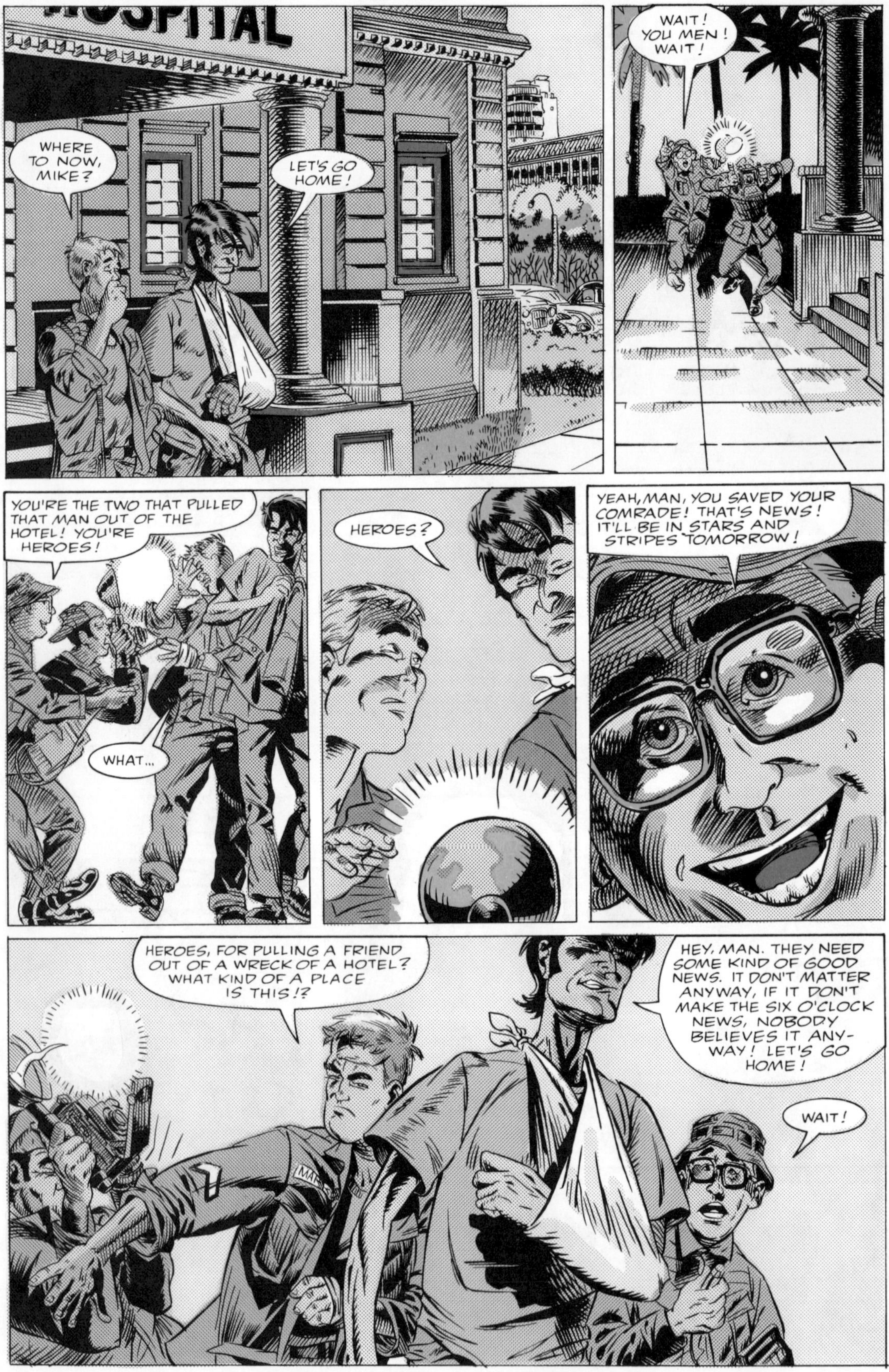
HOSPITAL
WHERE TO NOW, MIKE?
LET'S GO HOME!
WAIT! YOU MEN! WAIT!
YOU'RE THE TWO THAT PULLED THAT MAN OUT OF THE HOTEL! YOU'RE HEROES!
WHAT...
HEROES?
YEAH, MAN, YOU SAVED YOUR COMRADE! THAT'S NEWS! IT'LL BE IN STARS AND STRIPES TOMORROW!
HEROES, FOR PULLING A FRIEND OUT OF A WRECK OF A HOTEL? WHAT KIND OF A PLACE IS THIS!?
HEY, MAN. THEY NEED SOME KIND OF GOOD NEWS. IT DON'T MATTER ANYWAY, IF IT DON'T MAKE THE SIX O'CLOCK NEWS, NOBODY BELIEVES IT ANYWAY! LET'S GO HOME!
WAIT!

MIKE, SHOULD WE HAVE TALKED TO THAT GUY?
NAH. WE HELPED BECAUSE WE WANTED TO. DON'T LET 'EM MAKE ANYTHING ELSE OUT OF IT!
A SHORT TIME LATER...
INFANTRY
MECHANIZED, OF COURSE!
TOMAHAWKS
THAT'S IT, MAN. SAFE. HOME SWEET HOOCH.
YEAH, LET'S GET SOME SLEEP.
ROCKET ATTACK! EVERYBODY TO THE BUNKERS!
JEEZ, IF IT ISN'T ONE THING...

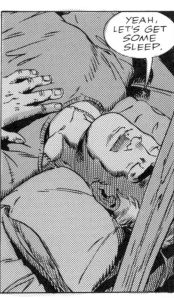

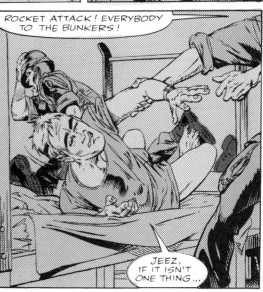

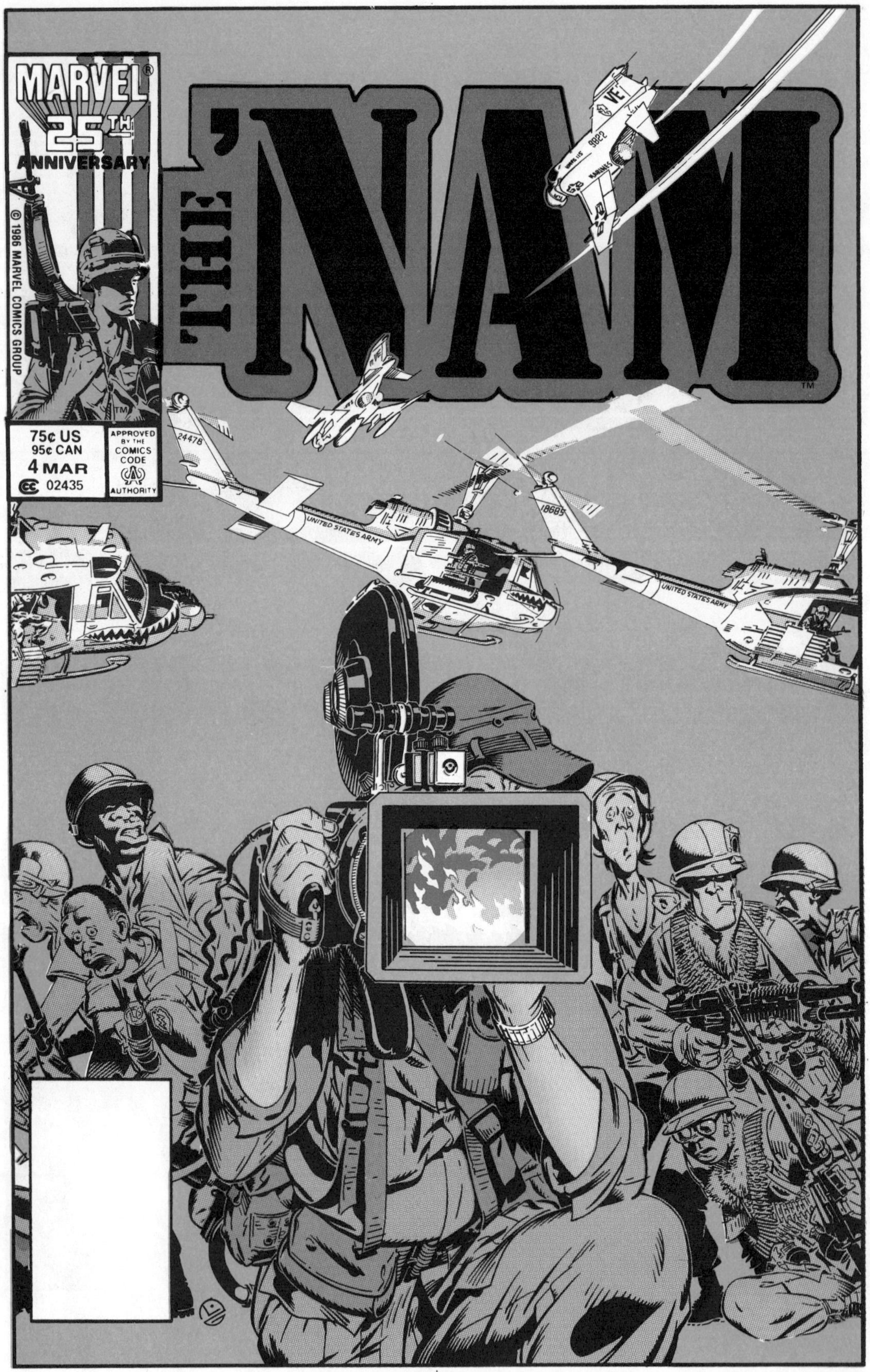
MARVEL
25TH
ANNIVERSARY
© 1986 MARVEL COMICS GROUP
THE 'NAM
75¢ US
95¢ CAN
4 MAR
02435
APPROVED BY THE COMICS CODE AUTHORITY
UNITED STATES ARMY
UNITED STATES ARMY

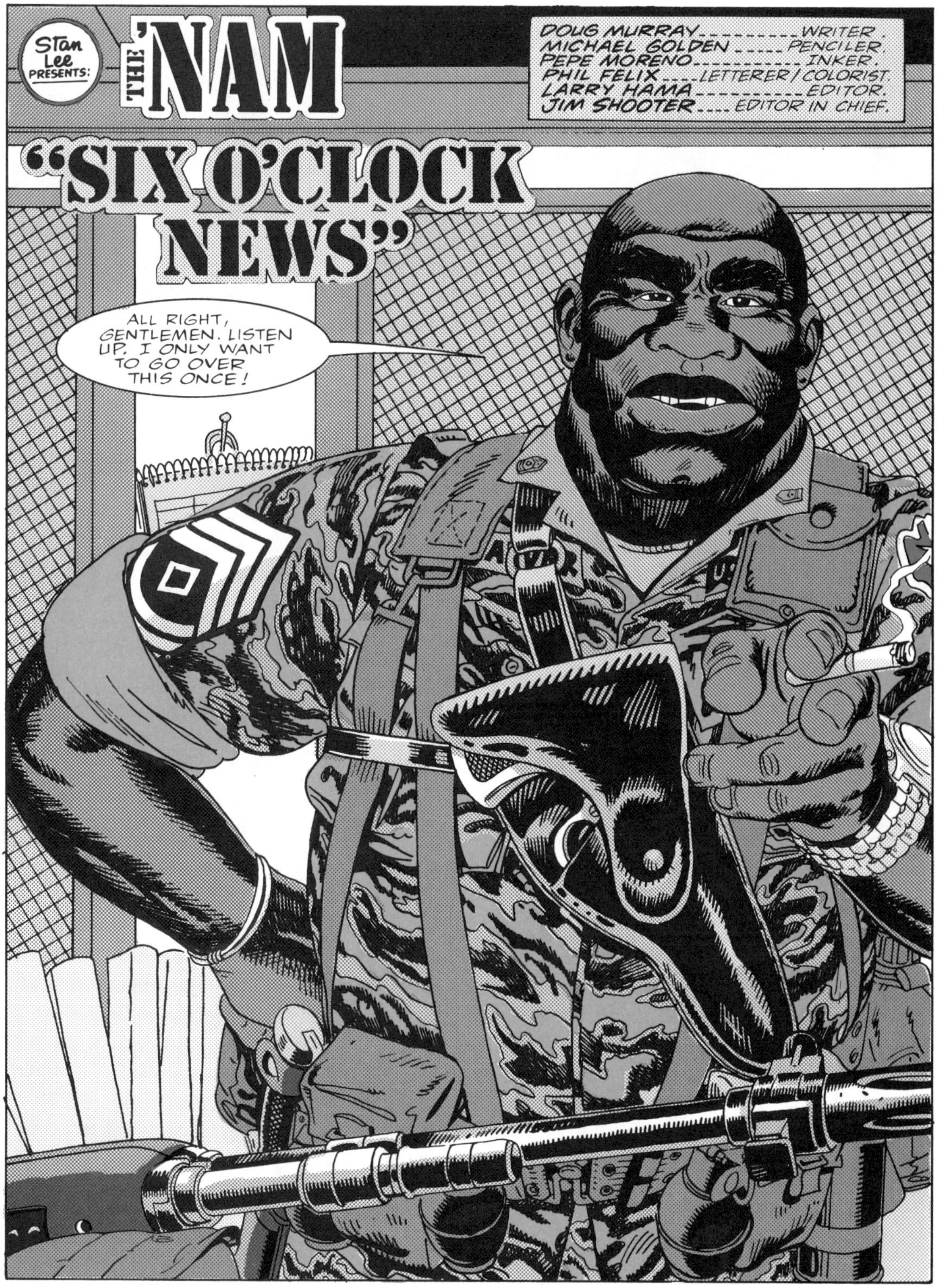
Stan Lee PRESENTS:
THE 'NAM
DOUG MURRAY..........WRITER
MICHAEL GOLDEN......PENCILER
PEPE MORENO..........INKER
PHIL FELIX....LETTERER / COLORIST
LARRY HAMA............EDITOR
JIM SHOOTER....EDITOR IN CHIEF
"SIX O'CLOCK NEWS"
ALL RIGHT, GENTLEMEN. LISTEN UP. I ONLY WANT TO GO OVER THIS ONCE!

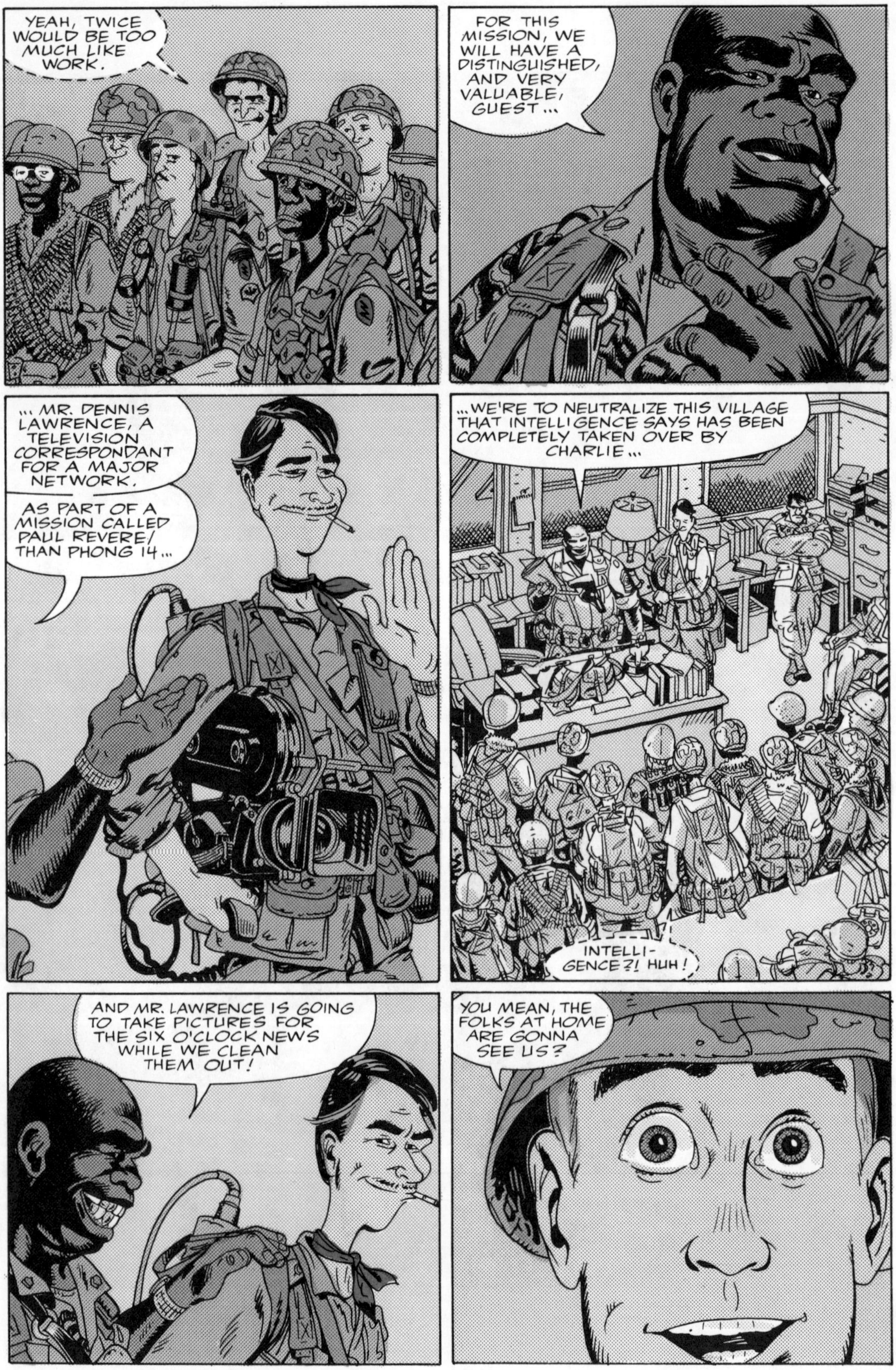
YEAH, TWICE WOULD BE TOO MUCH LIKE WORK.
FOR THIS MISSION, WE WILL HAVE A DISTINGUISHED, AND VERY VALUABLE, GUEST...
...MR. DENNIS LAWRENCE, A TELEVISION CORRESPONDANT FOR A MAJOR NETWORK.
AS PART OF A MISSION CALLED PAUL REVERE/ THAN PHONG 14...
...WE'RE TO NEUTRALIZE THIS VILLAGE THAT INTELLIGENCE SAYS HAS BEEN COMPLETELY TAKEN OVER BY CHARLIE...
INTELLI- GENCE?! HUH!
AND MR. LAWRENCE IS GOING TO TAKE PICTURES FOR THE SIX O'CLOCK NEWS WHILE WE CLEAN THEM OUT!
YOU MEAN, THE FOLKS AT HOME ARE GONNA SEE US?

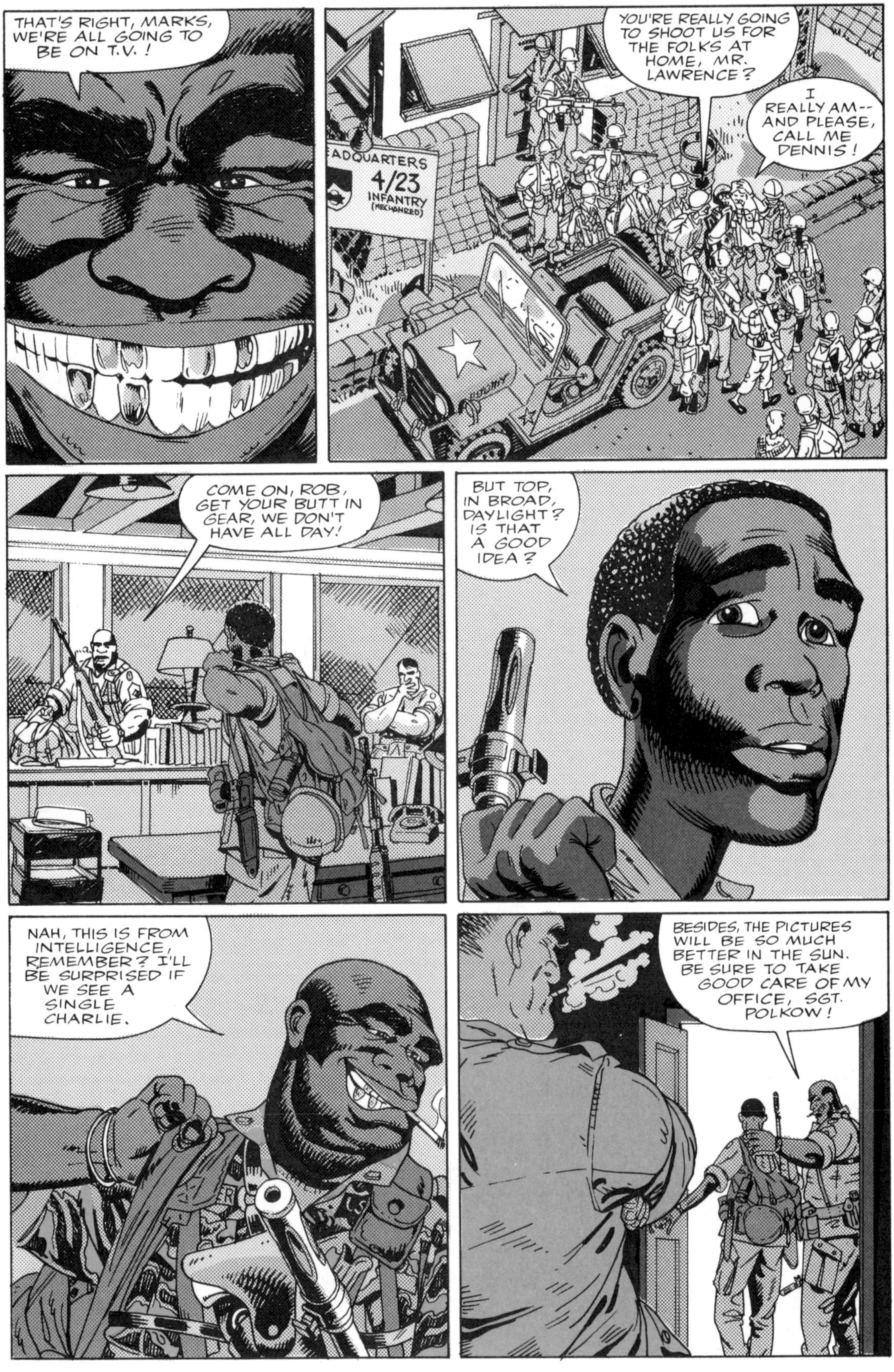
THAT'S RIGHT, MARKS, WE'RE ALL GOING TO BE ON T.V.!
YOU'RE REALLY GOING TO SHOOT US FOR THE FOLKS AT HOME, MR. LAWRENCE?
I REALLY AM-- AND PLEASE, CALL ME DENNIS!
EADQUARTERS 4/23 INFANTRY (MECHANIZED)
COME ON, ROB, GET YOUR BUTT IN GEAR, WE DON'T HAVE ALL DAY!
BUT TOP, IN BROAD DAYLIGHT? IS THAT A GOOD IDEA?
NAH, THIS IS FROM INTELLIGENCE, REMEMBER? I'LL BE SURPRISED IF WE SEE A SINGLE CHARLIE.
BESIDES, THE PICTURES WILL BE SO MUCH BETTER IN THE SUN. BE SURE TO TAKE GOOD CARE OF MY OFFICE, SGT. POLKOW!

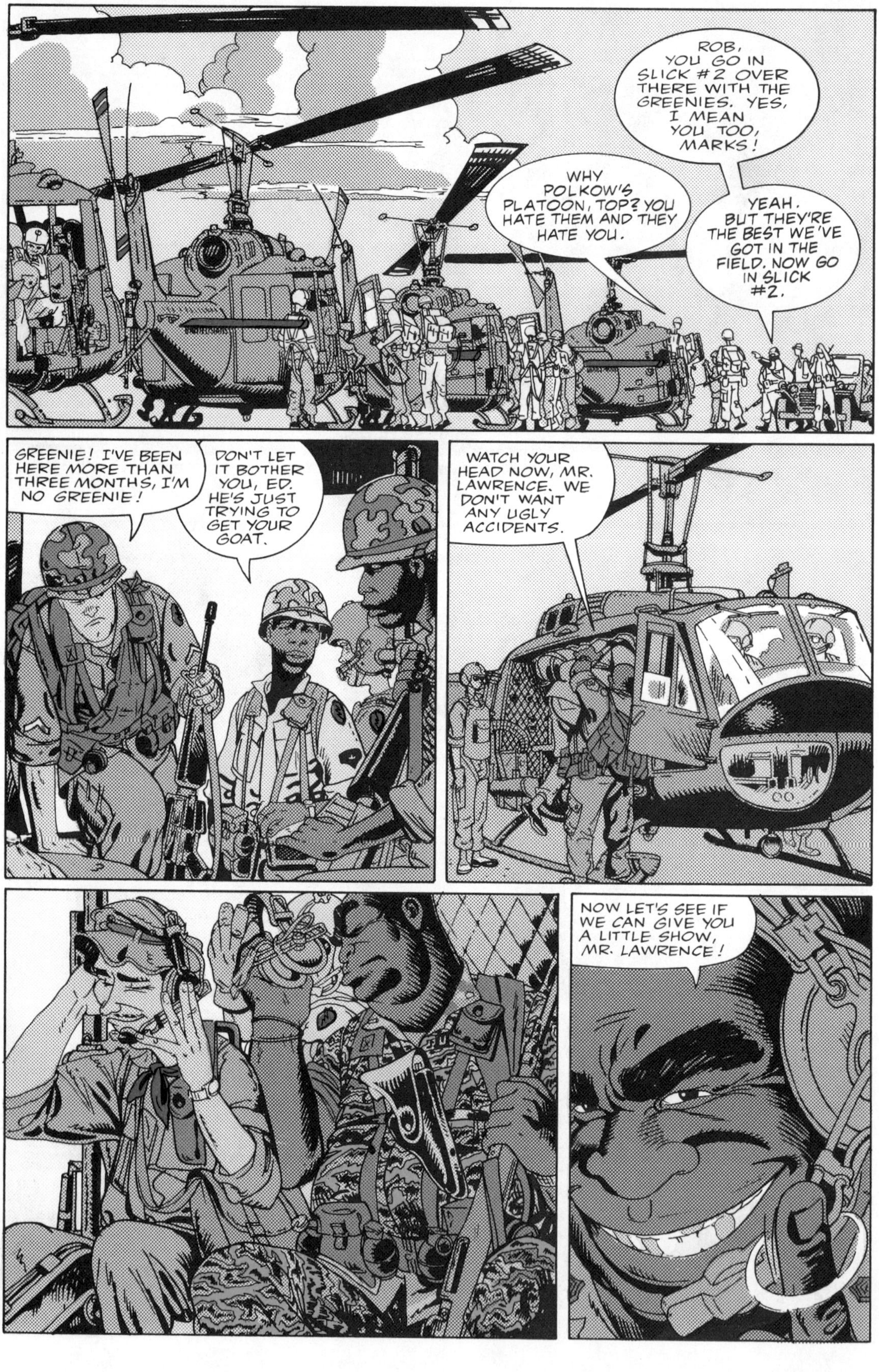
ROB, YOU GO IN SLICK #2 OVER THERE WITH THE GREENIES. YES, I MEAN YOU TOO, MARKS!
WHY POLKOW'S PLATOON, TOP? YOU HATE THEM AND THEY HATE YOU.
YEAH. BUT THEY'RE THE BEST WE'VE GOT IN THE FIELD. NOW GO IN SLICK #2.
GREENIE! I'VE BEEN HERE MORE THAN THREE MONTHS, I'M NO GREENIE!
DON'T LET IT BOTHER YOU, ED. HE'S JUST TRYING TO GET YOUR GOAT.
WATCH YOUR HEAD NOW, MR. LAWRENCE. WE DON'T WANT ANY UGLY ACCIDENTS.
NOW LET'S SEE IF WE CAN GIVE YOU A LITTLE SHOW, MR. LAWRENCE!

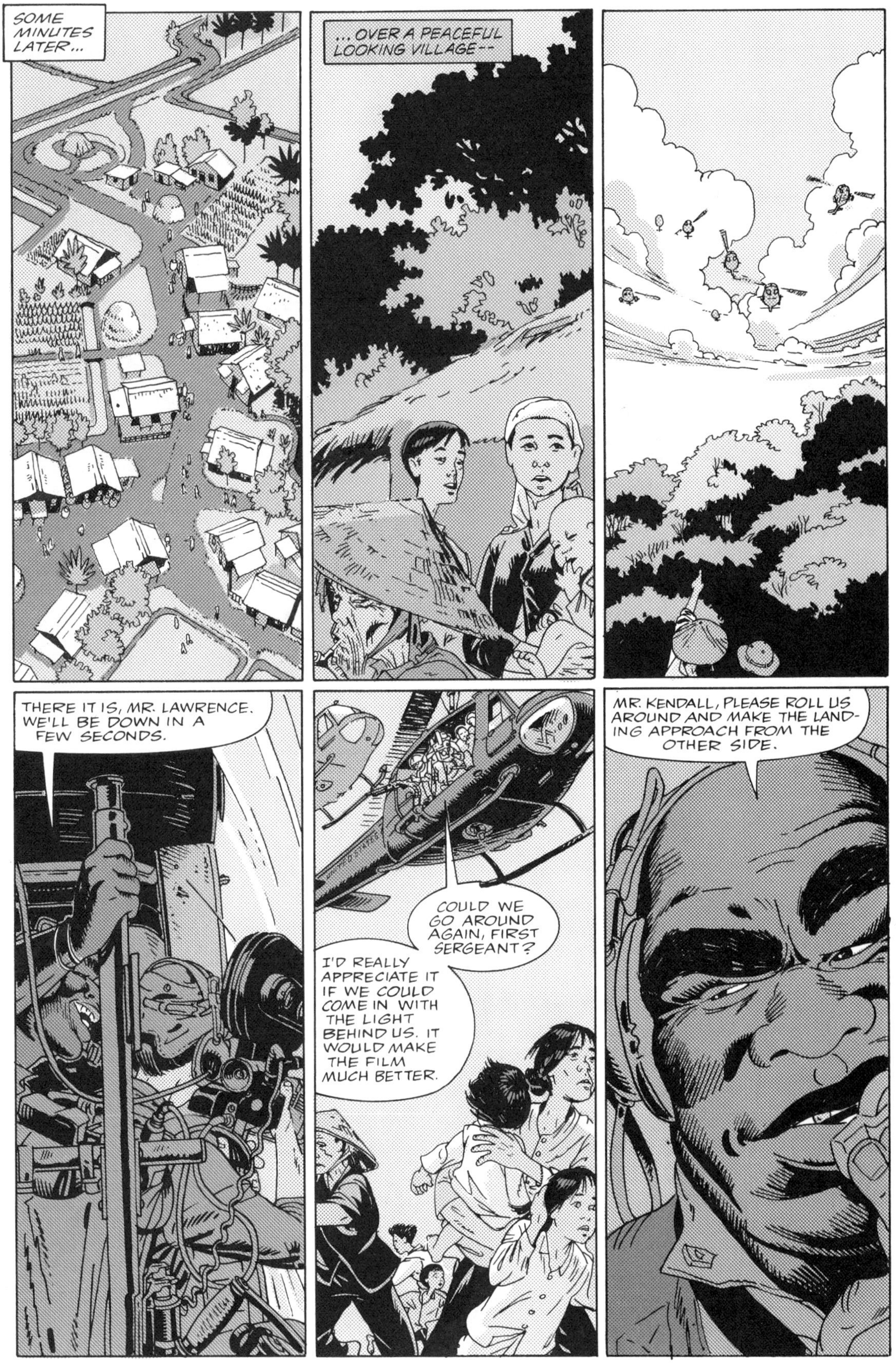
SOME MINUTES LATER...
...OVER A PEACEFUL LOOKING VILLAGE--
THERE IT IS, MR. LAWRENCE. WE'LL BE DOWN IN A FEW SECONDS.
COULD WE GO AROUND AGAIN, FIRST SERGEANT?
I'D REALLY APPRECIATE IT IF WE COULD COME IN WITH THE LIGHT BEHIND US. IT WOULD MAKE THE FILM MUCH BETTER.
MR. KENDALL, PLEASE ROLL US AROUND AND MAKE THE LANDING APPROACH FROM THE OTHER SIDE.

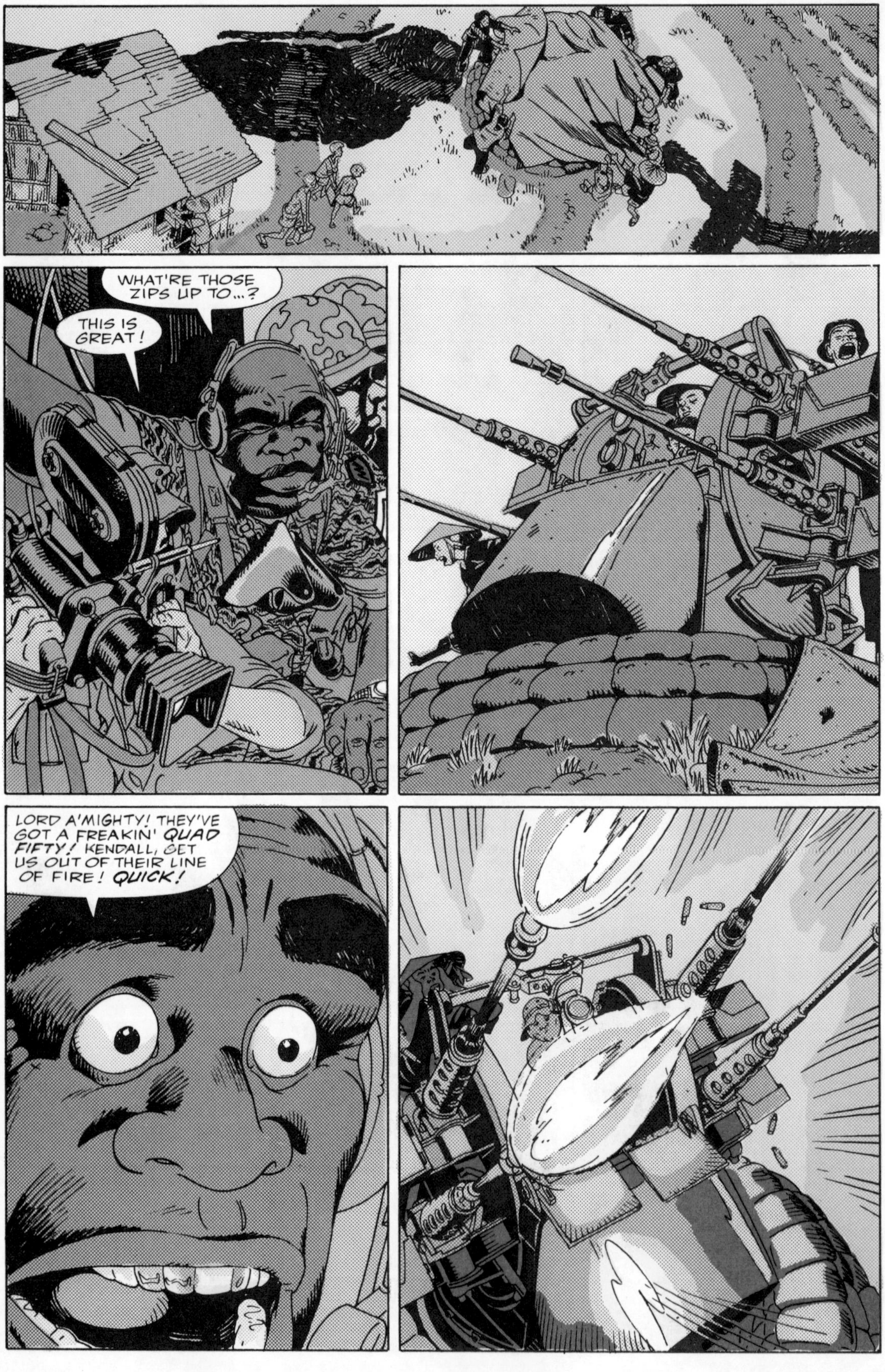
WHAT'RE THOSE ZIPS UP TO...?
THIS IS GREAT!
LORD A'MIGHTY! THEY'VE GOT A FREAKIN' *QUAD FIFTY!* KENDALL, GET US OUT OF THEIR LINE OF FIRE! *QUICK!*

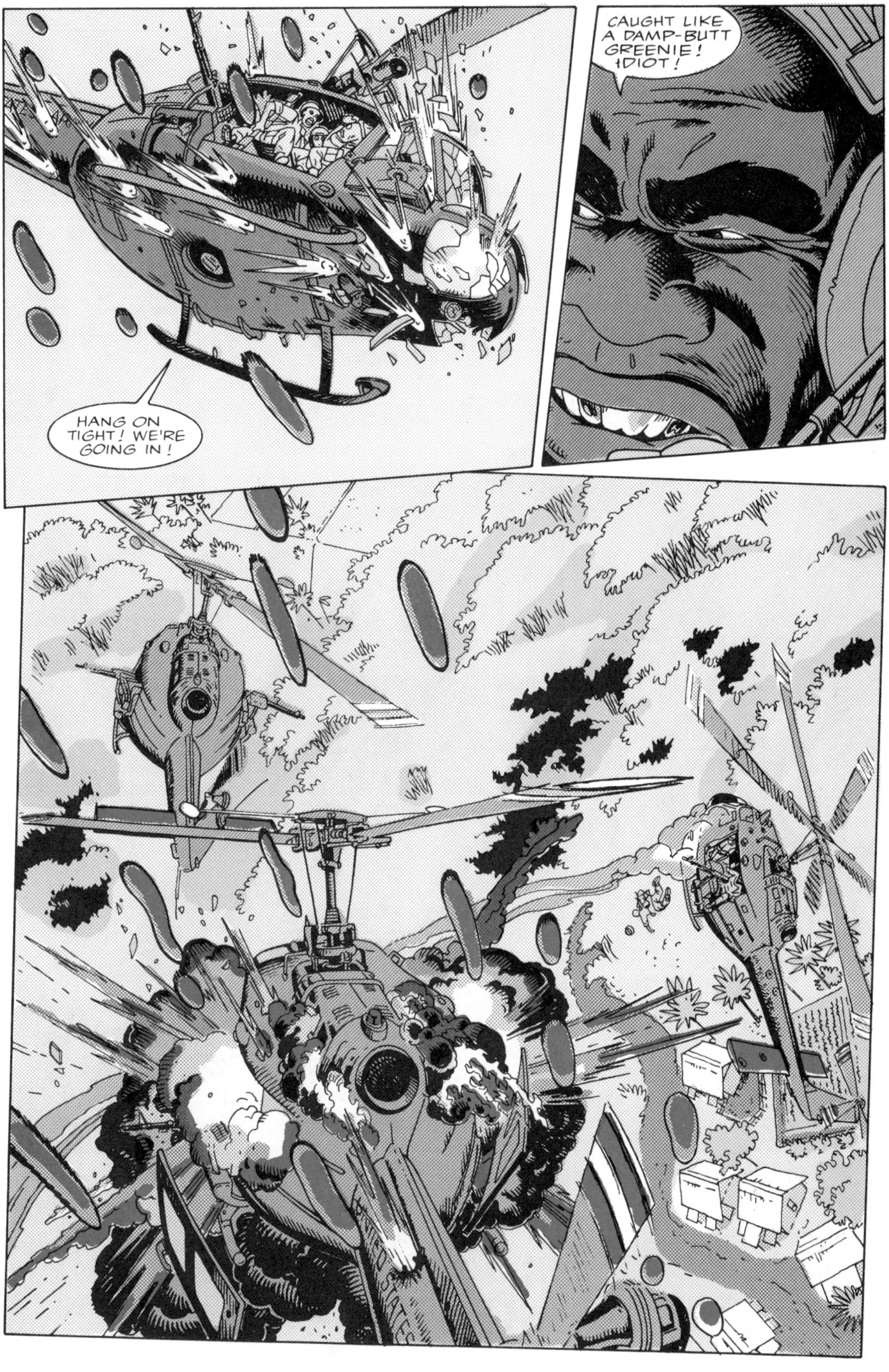
HANG ON TIGHT! WE'RE GOING IN!
CAUGHT LIKE A DAMP-BUTT GREENIE! IDIOT!

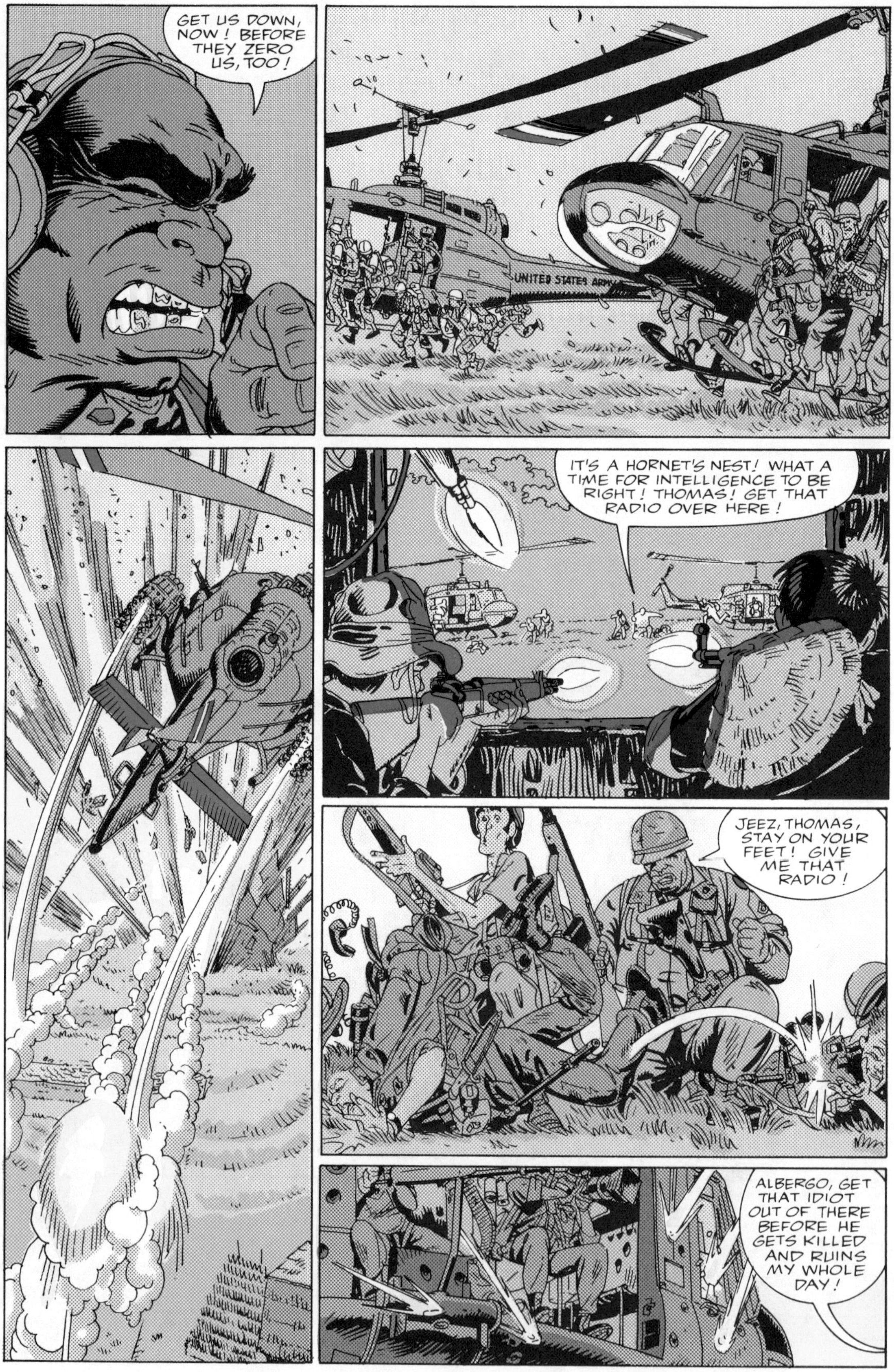
GET US DOWN, NOW! BEFORE THEY ZERO US, TOO!
UNITED STATES ARMY
IT'S A HORNET'S NEST! WHAT A TIME FOR INTELLIGENCE TO BE RIGHT! THOMAS! GET THAT RADIO OVER HERE!
JEEZ, THOMAS, STAY ON YOUR FEET! GIVE ME THAT RADIO!
ALBERGO, GET THAT IDIOT OUT OF THERE BEFORE HE GETS KILLED AND RUINS MY WHOLE DAY!

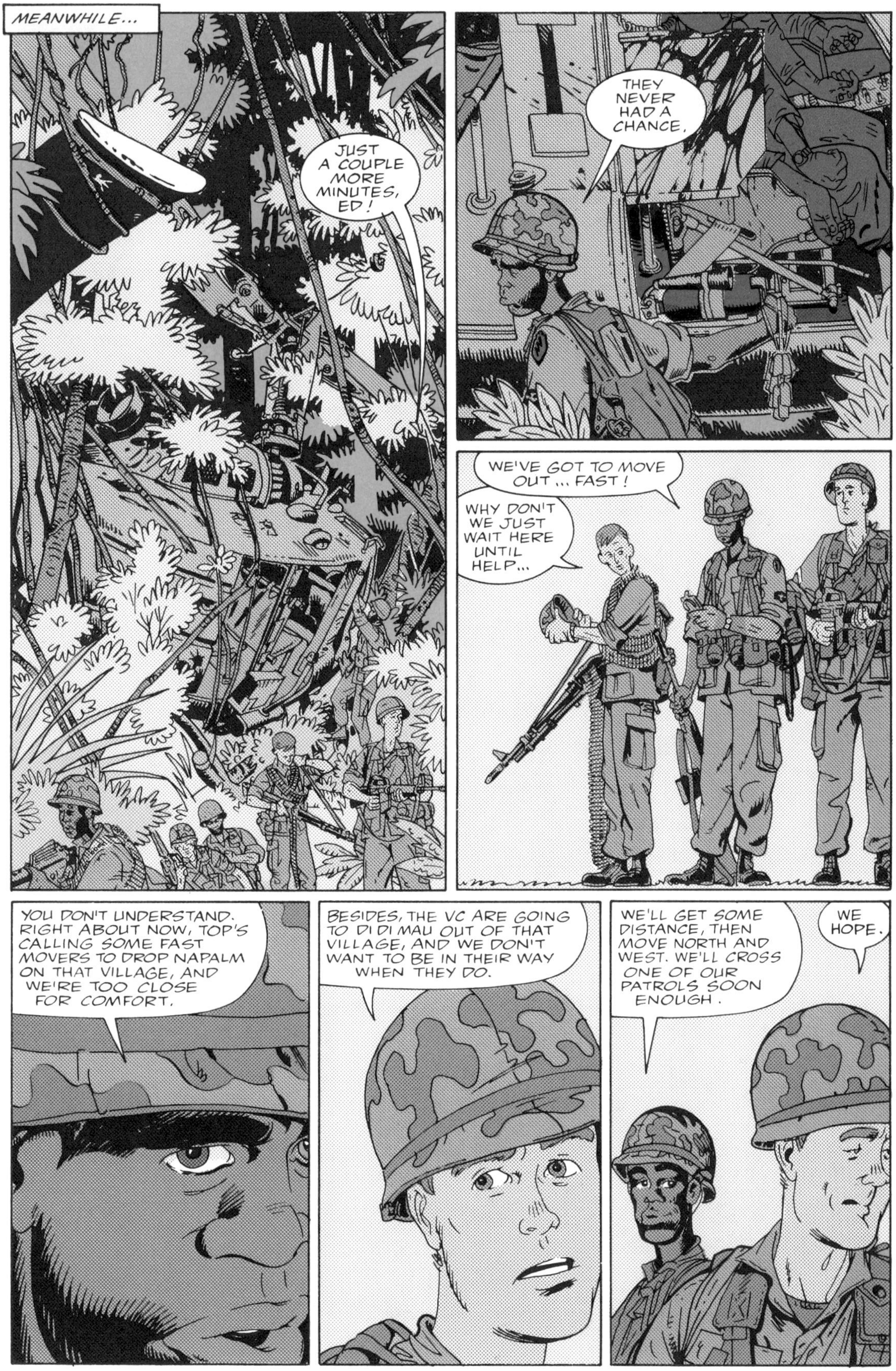
MEANWHILE...
JUST A COUPLE MORE MINUTES, ED!
THEY NEVER HAD A CHANCE.
WE'VE GOT TO MOVE OUT... FAST!
WHY DON'T WE JUST WAIT HERE UNTIL HELP...
YOU DON'T UNDERSTAND. RIGHT ABOUT NOW, TOP'S CALLING SOME FAST MOVERS TO DROP NAPALM ON THAT VILLAGE, AND WE'RE TOO CLOSE FOR COMFORT.
BESIDES, THE VC ARE GOING TO DI DI MAU OUT OF THAT VILLAGE, AND WE DON'T WANT TO BE IN THEIR WAY WHEN THEY DO.
WE'LL GET SOME DISTANCE, THEN MOVE NORTH AND WEST. WE'LL CROSS ONE OF OUR PATROLS SOON ENOUGH.
WE HOPE.

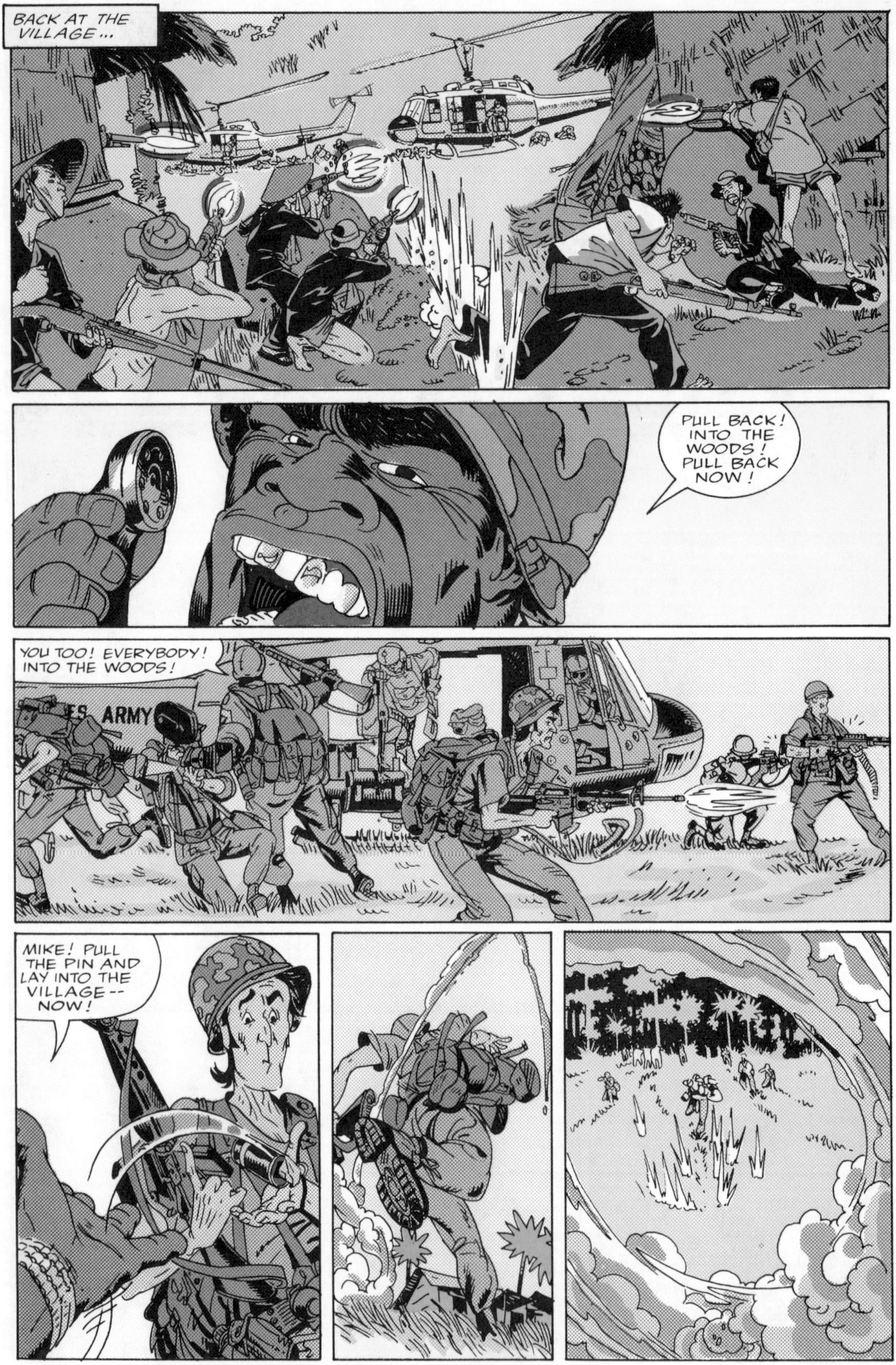
BACK AT THE VILLAGE...
PULL BACK! INTO THE WOODS! PULL BACK NOW!
YOU TOO! EVERYBODY! INTO THE WOODS!
ARMY
MIKE! PULL THE PIN AND LAY INTO THE VILLAGE -- NOW!

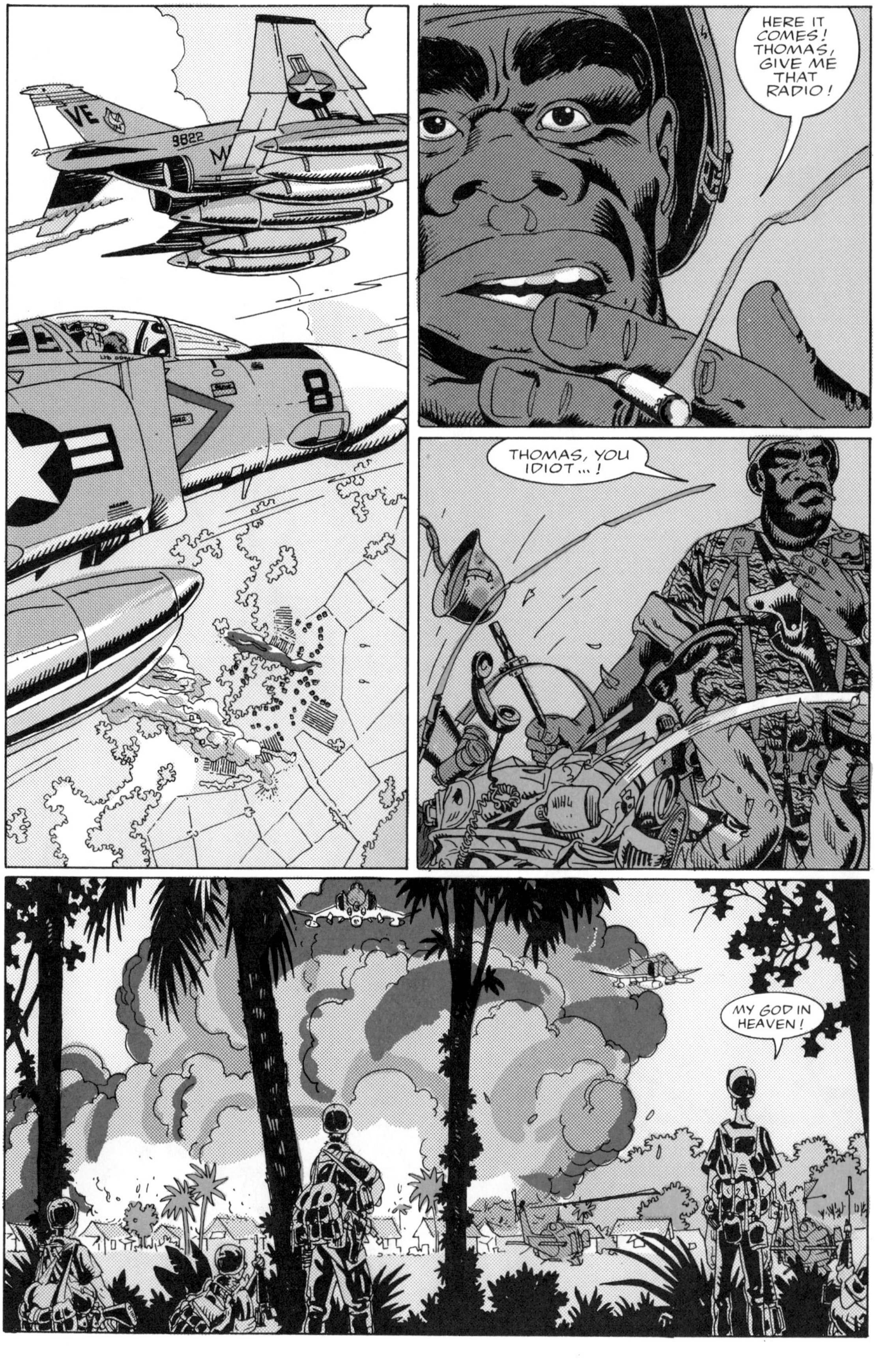
VE
9822
8
HERE IT COMES! THOMAS, GIVE ME THAT RADIO!
THOMAS, YOU IDIOT...!
MY GOD IN HEAVEN!

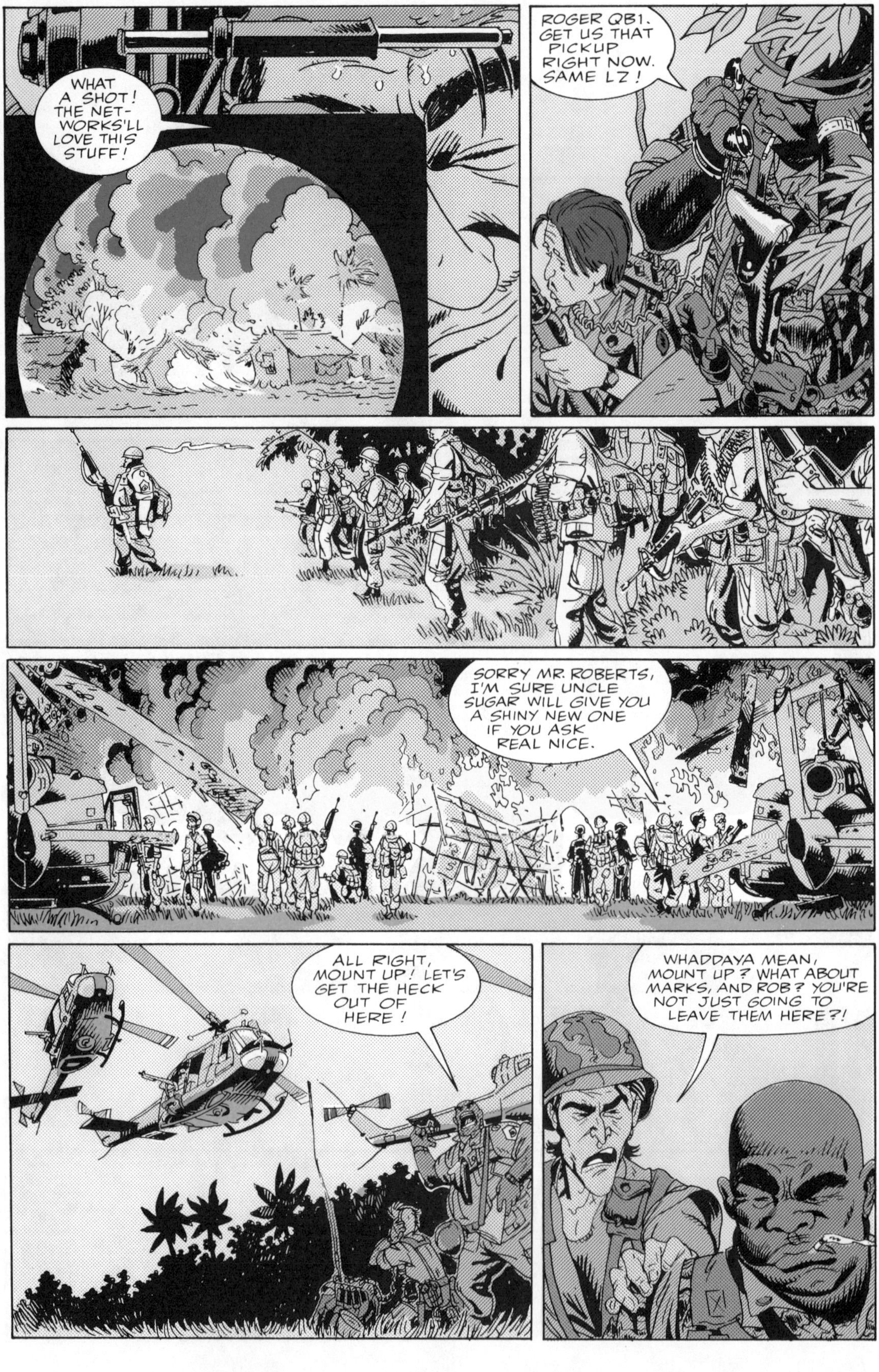
WHAT A SHOT! THE NET-WORKS'LL LOVE THIS STUFF!
ROGER QB1. GET US THAT PICKUP RIGHT NOW. SAME LZ!
SORRY MR. ROBERTS, I'M SURE UNCLE SUGAR WILL GIVE YOU A SHINY NEW ONE IF YOU ASK REAL NICE.
ALL RIGHT, MOUNT UP! LET'S GET THE HECK OUT OF HERE!
WHADDAYA MEAN, MOUNT UP? WHAT ABOUT MARKS, AND ROB? YOU'RE NOT JUST GOING TO LEAVE THEM HERE?!

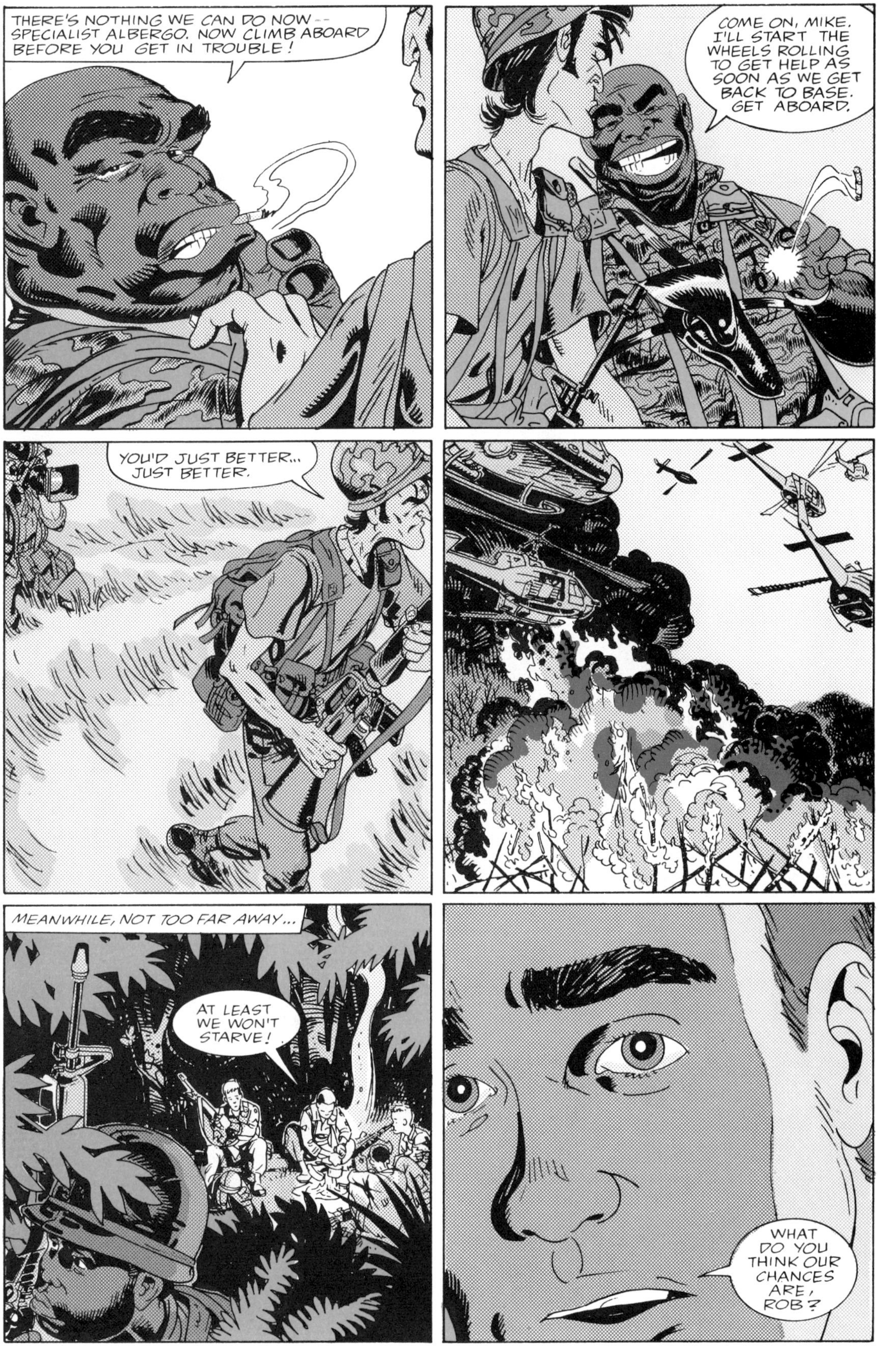
THERE'S NOTHING WE CAN DO NOW-- SPECIALIST ALBERGO. NOW CLIMB ABOARD BEFORE YOU GET IN TROUBLE!
COME ON, MIKE. I'LL START THE WHEELS ROLLING TO GET HELP AS SOON AS WE GET BACK TO BASE. GET ABOARD.
YOU'D JUST BETTER... JUST BETTER.
MEANWHILE, NOT TOO FAR AWAY...
AT LEAST WE WON'T STARVE!
WHAT DO YOU THINK OUR CHANCES ARE, ROB?

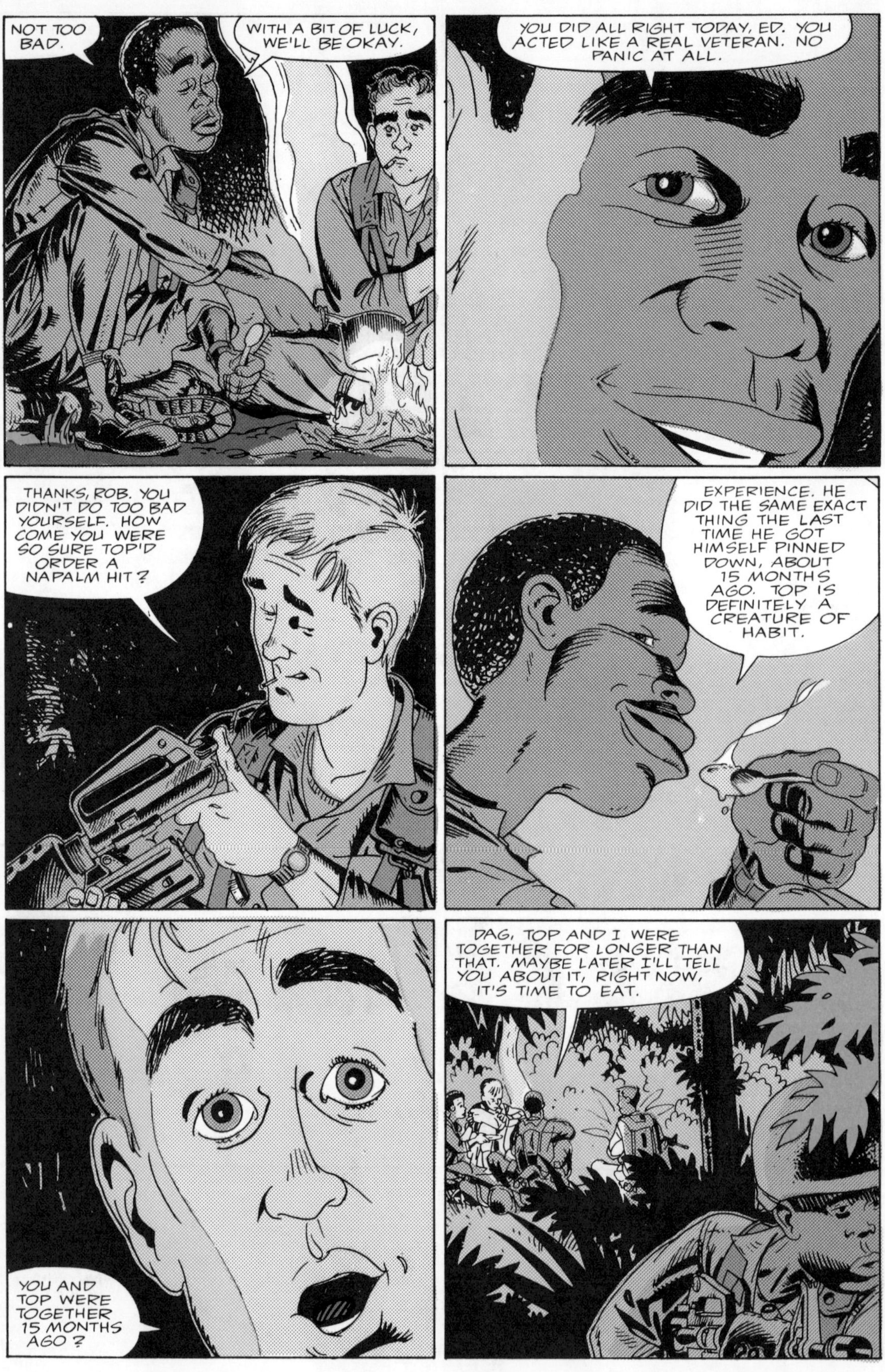
NOT TOO BAD.
WITH A BIT OF LUCK, WE'LL BE OKAY.
YOU DID ALL RIGHT TODAY, ED. YOU ACTED LIKE A REAL VETERAN. NO PANIC AT ALL.
THANKS, ROB. YOU DIDN'T DO TOO BAD YOURSELF. HOW COME YOU WERE SO SURE TOP'D ORDER A NAPALM HIT?
EXPERIENCE. HE DID THE SAME EXACT THING THE LAST TIME HE GOT HIMSELF PINNED DOWN, ABOUT 15 MONTHS AGO. TOP IS DEFINITELY A CREATURE OF HABIT.
YOU AND TOP WERE TOGETHER 15 MONTHS AGO?
DAG, TOP AND I WERE TOGETHER FOR LONGER THAN THAT. MAYBE LATER I'LL TELL YOU ABOUT IT, RIGHT NOW, IT'S TIME TO EAT.

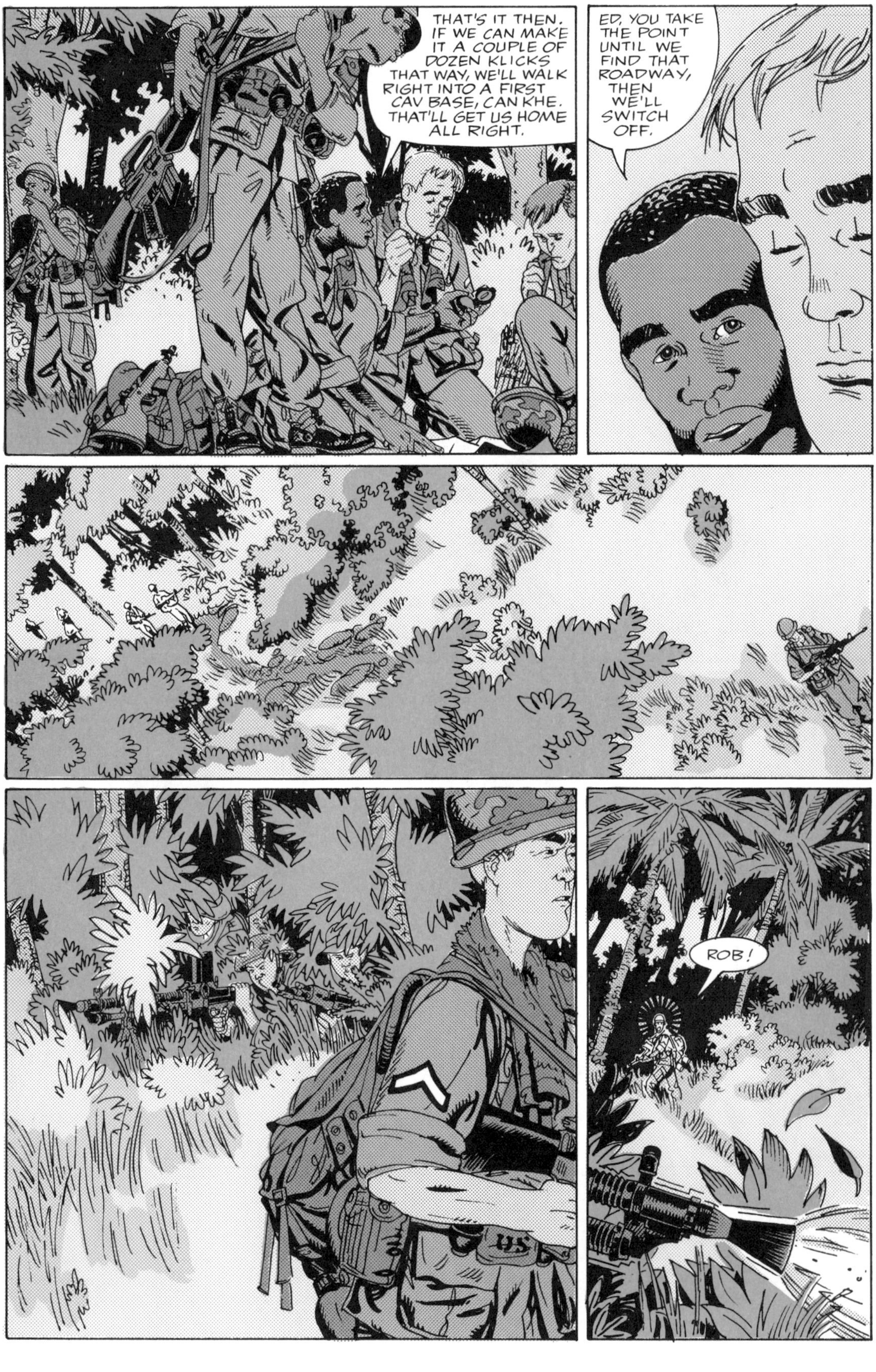
THAT'S IT THEN. IF WE CAN MAKE IT A COUPLE OF DOZEN KLICKS THAT WAY, WE'LL WALK RIGHT INTO A FIRST CAV BASE, CAN KHE. THAT'LL GET US HOME ALL RIGHT.
ED, YOU TAKE THE POINT UNTIL WE FIND THAT ROADWAY, THEN WE'LL SWITCH OFF.
ROB!

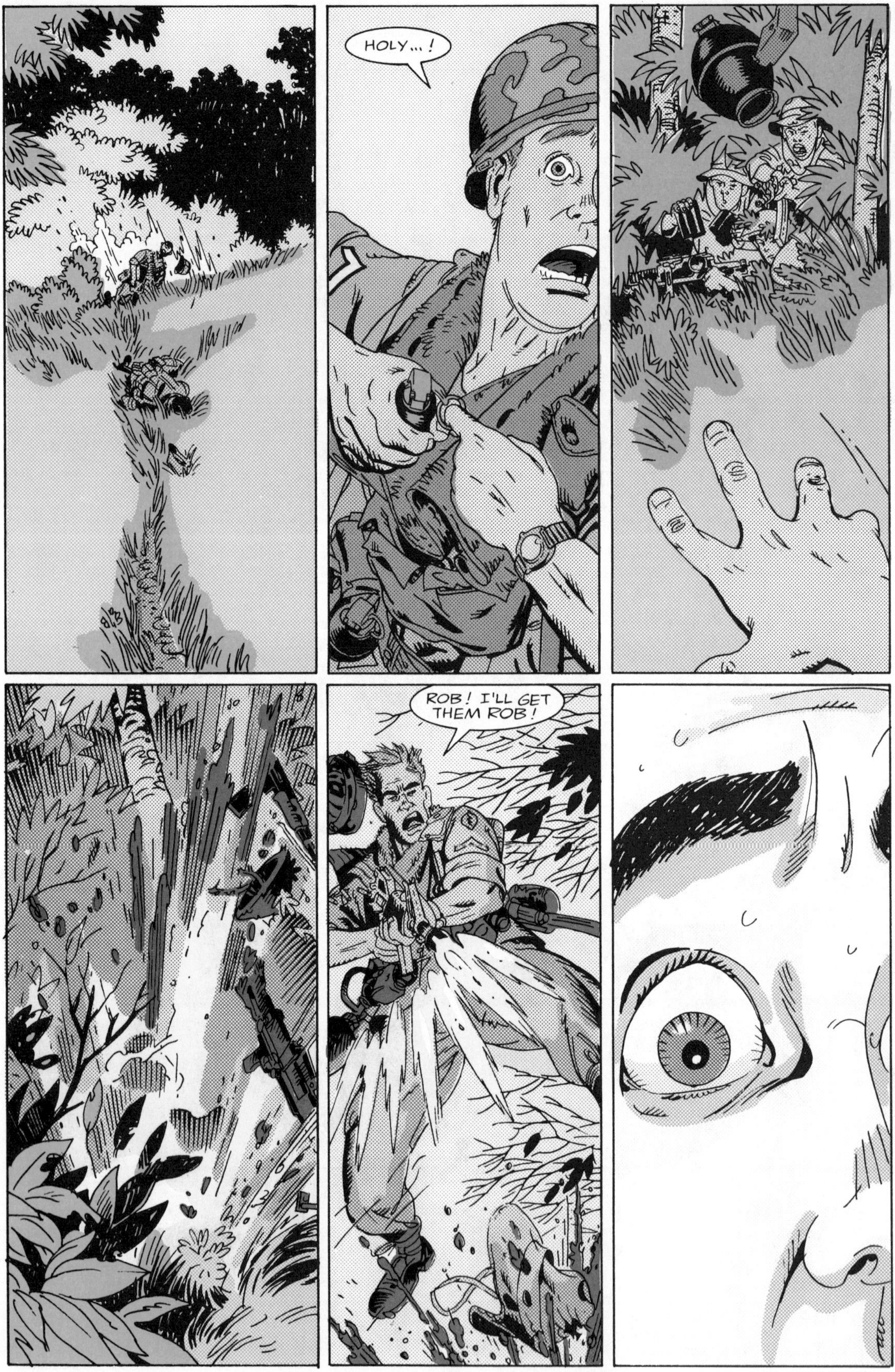
HOLY...!
ROB! I'LL GET THEM ROB!

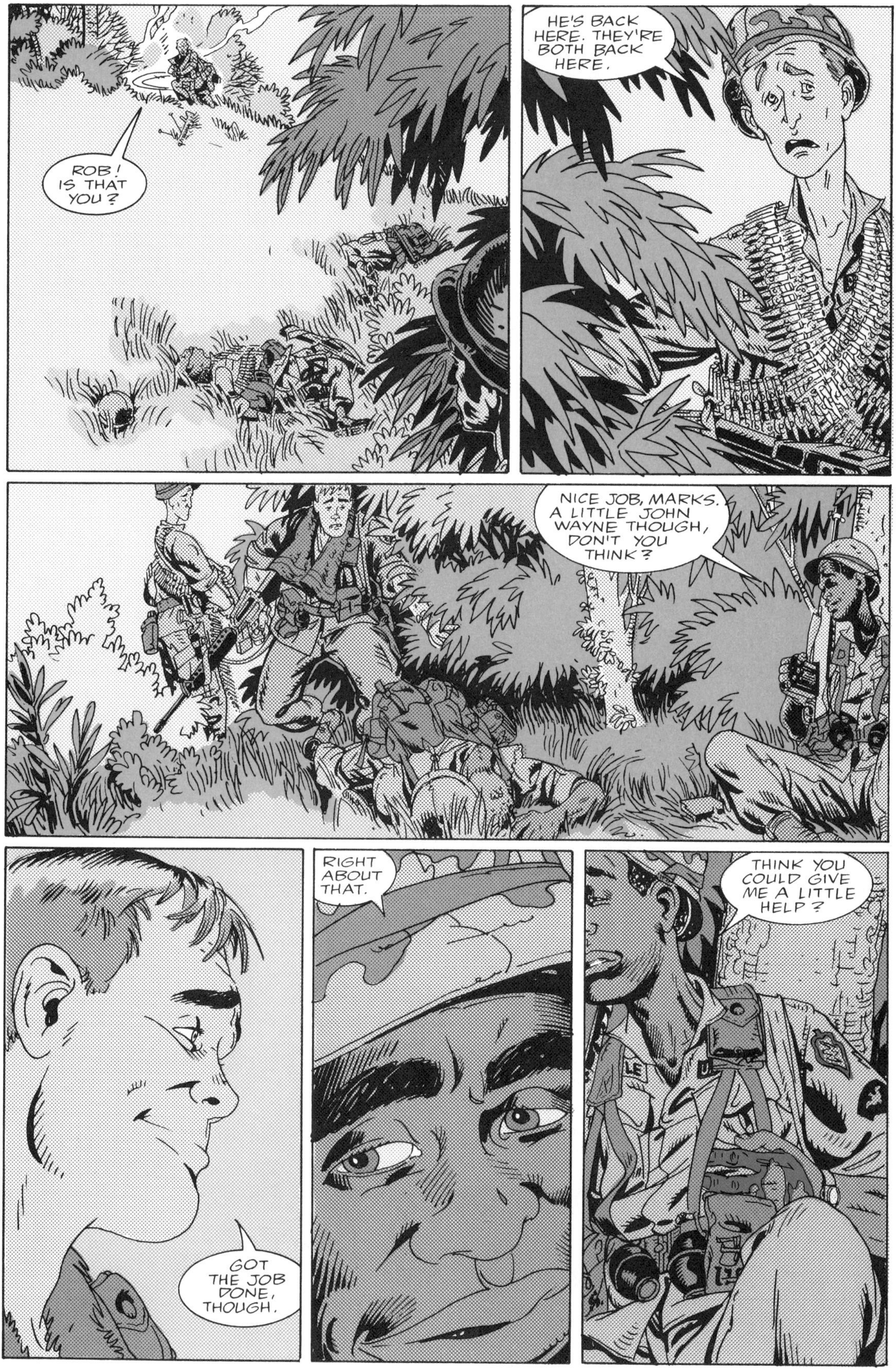
ROB! IS THAT YOU?
HE'S BACK HERE. THEY'RE BOTH BACK HERE.
NICE JOB, MARKS. A LITTLE JOHN WAYNE THOUGH, DON'T YOU THINK?
GOT THE JOB DONE, THOUGH.
RIGHT ABOUT THAT.
THINK YOU COULD GIVE ME A LITTLE HELP?

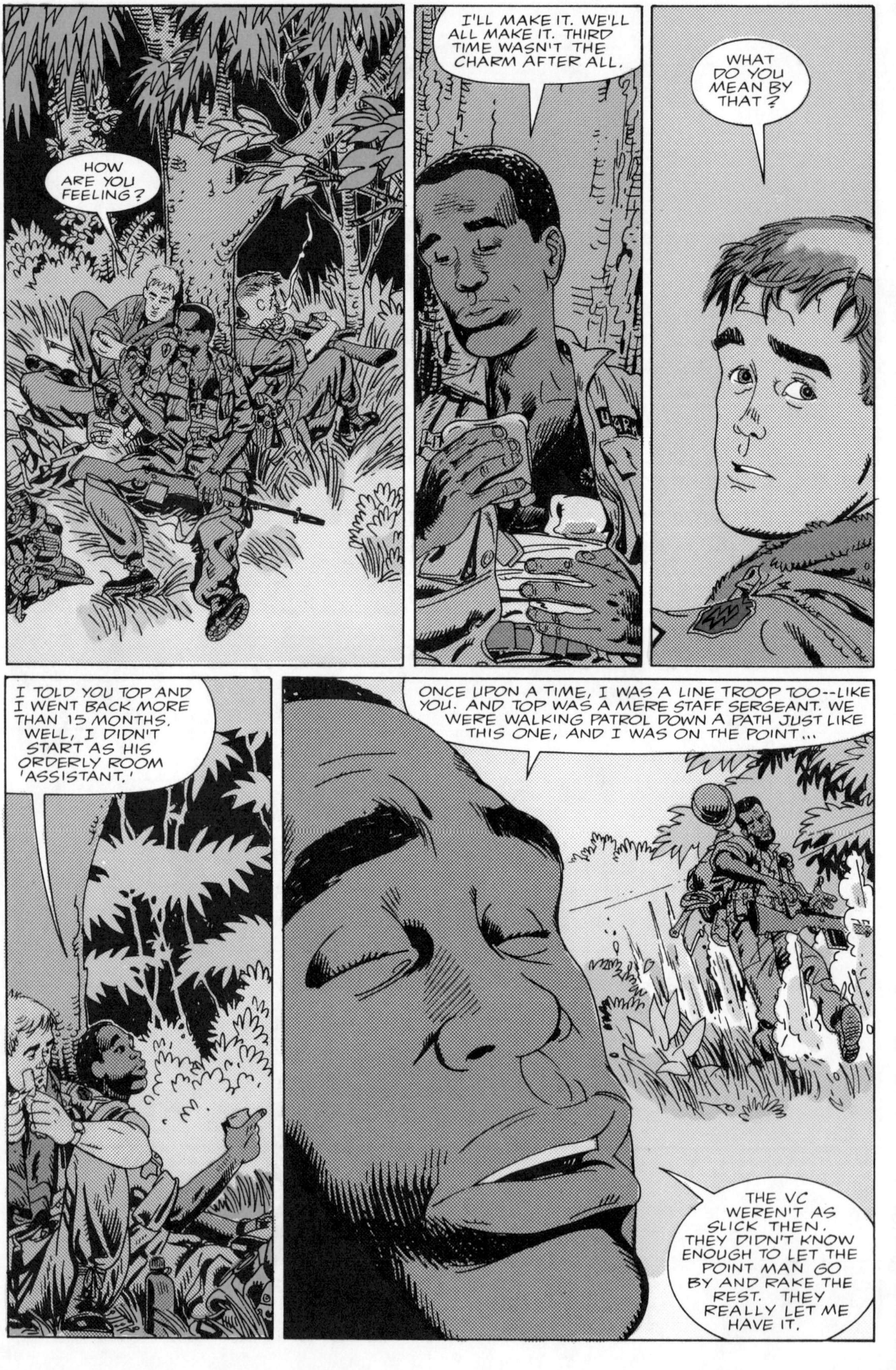
HOW ARE YOU FEELING?
I'LL MAKE IT. WE'LL ALL MAKE IT. THIRD TIME WASN'T THE CHARM AFTER ALL.
WHAT DO YOU MEAN BY THAT?
I TOLD YOU TOP AND I WENT BACK MORE THAN 15 MONTHS. WELL, I DIDN'T START AS HIS ORDERLY ROOM 'ASSISTANT.'
ONCE UPON A TIME, I WAS A LINE TROOP TOO--LIKE YOU. AND TOP WAS A MERE STAFF SERGEANT. WE WERE WALKING PATROL DOWN A PATH JUST LIKE THIS ONE, AND I WAS ON THE POINT...
THE VC WEREN'T AS SLICK THEN. THEY DIDN'T KNOW ENOUGH TO LET THE POINT MAN GO BY AND RAKE THE REST. THEY REALLY LET ME HAVE IT.

"I GOT HIT PRETTY BAD, AND JIMBO, THAT'S WHAT WE CALLED TOP BACK THEN, JUST CHARGED RIGHT IN AND CUT THOSE VC TO PIECES."

TIME I GOT OUT OF THE HOSPITAL, JIMBO HAD MADE FIRST SERGEANT AT THE 23RD. I RE-UPPED FOR ANOTHER TOUR AND GOT STATIONED WITH HIM. COUPLE OF MONTHS LATER, I GOT HIT BY A SNIPER NOT TWENTY KLICKS FROM THE BASE...

THE ARMY FIGURES THAT THIRD TIME'S THE CHARM. IF YOU GET TWO PURPLE HEARTS, THEY PUT YOU ON A DESK. SO I ENDED UP AS JIMBO'S FLUNKY. AND THE WAR CHANGED HIM. MADE HIM MERCENARY, GRABBY, SOUR... I DON'T KNOW.

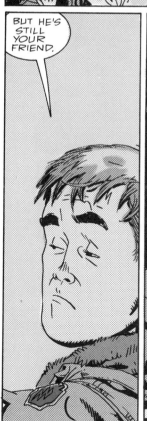

BUT HE'S STILL YOUR FRIEND.

YEAH, I GUESS HE IS. WONDER WHAT HE'LL DO NOW THAT I'VE COPPED NUMBER THREE?

LET'S WORRY ABOUT THAT AFTER WE GET HOME, SHALL WE? NOW, IF WE GO THIS WAY TOMORROW...

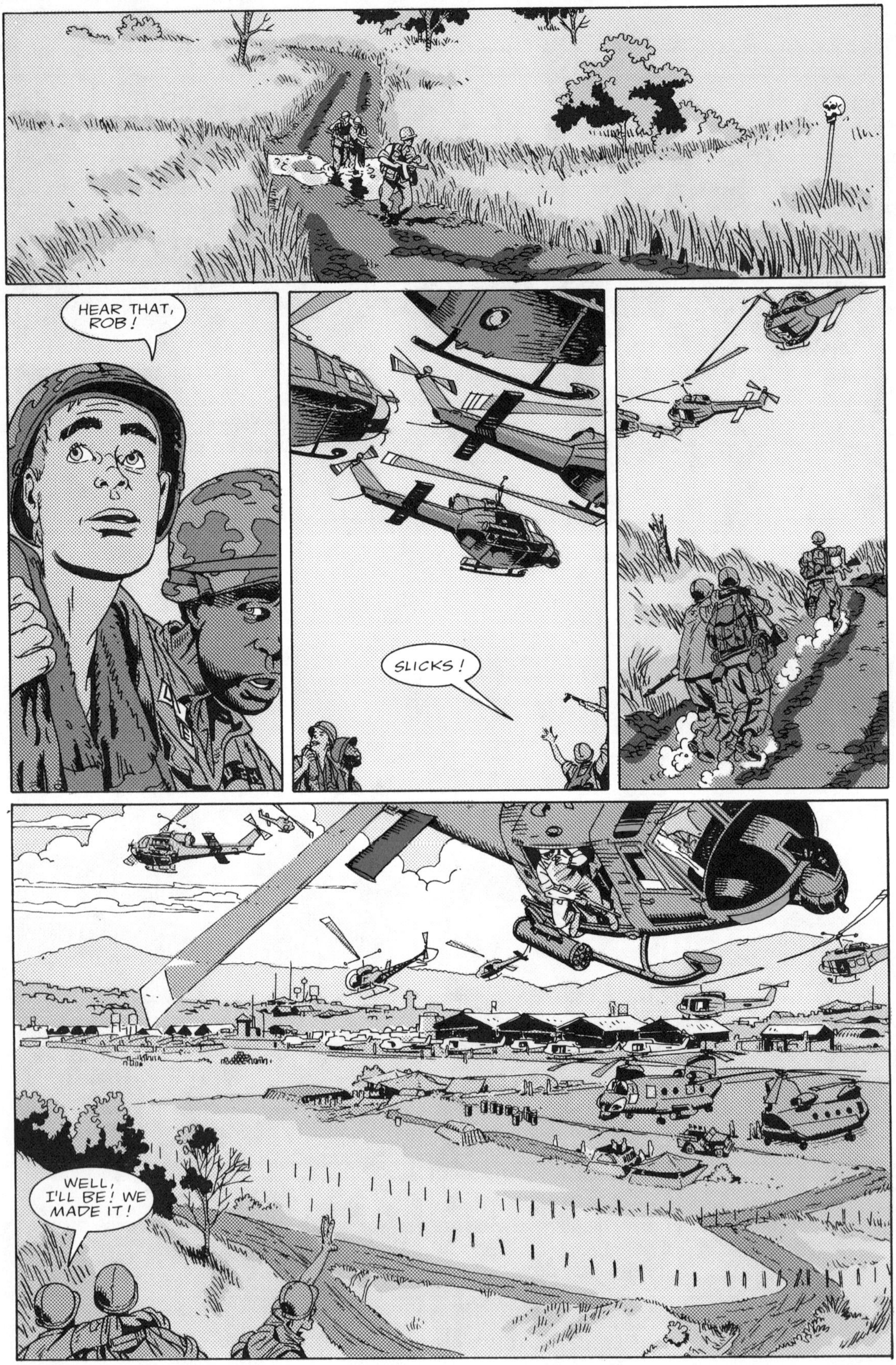
HEAR THAT, ROB!
SLICKS!
WELL, I'LL BE! WE MADE IT!

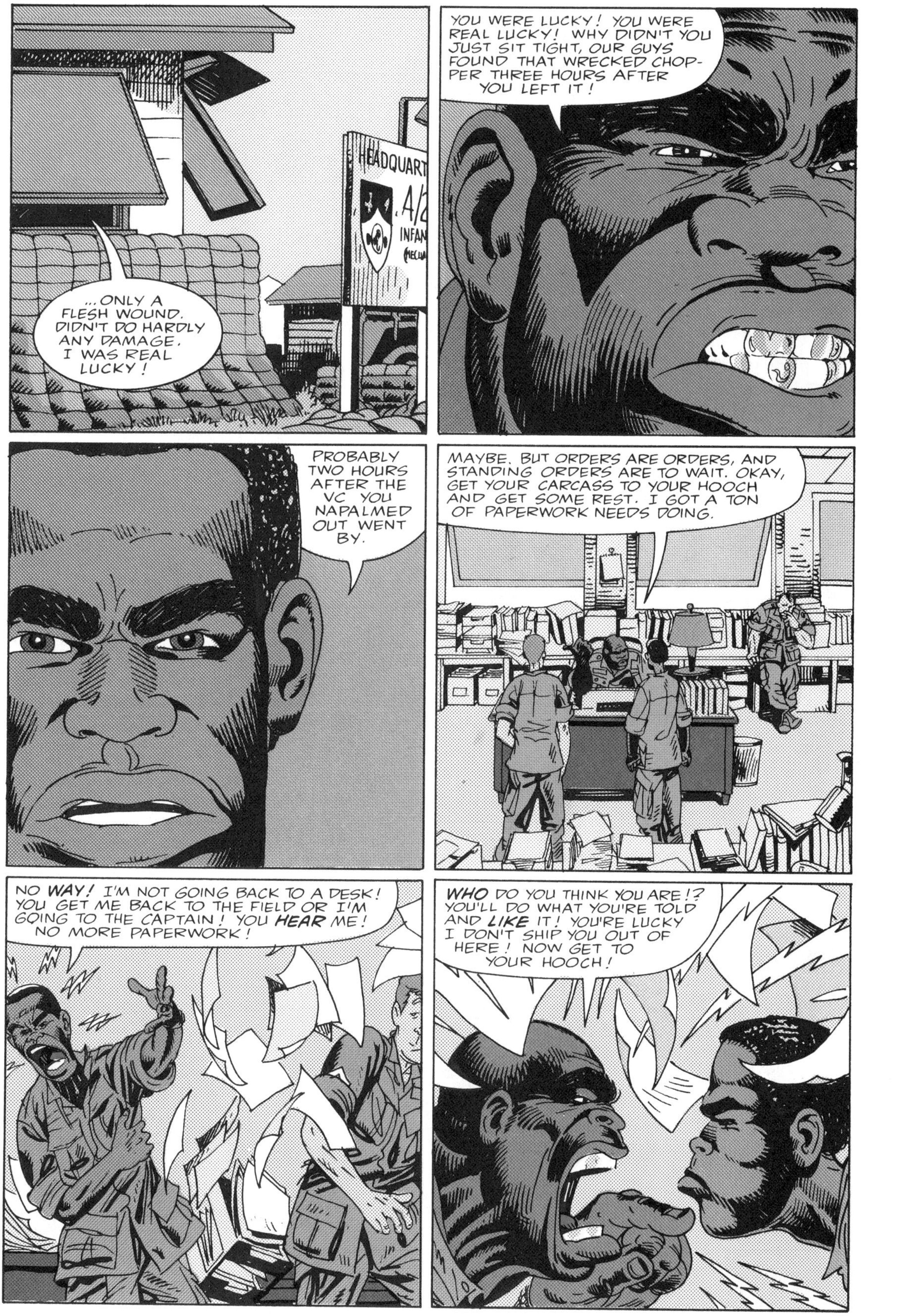
...ONLY A FLESH WOUND. DIDN'T DO HARDLY ANY DAMAGE. I WAS REAL LUCKY!
HEADQUART
4/2
INFAN
YOU WERE LUCKY! YOU WERE REAL LUCKY! WHY DIDN'T YOU JUST SIT TIGHT, OUR GUYS FOUND THAT WRECKED CHOPPER THREE HOURS AFTER YOU LEFT IT!
PROBABLY TWO HOURS AFTER THE VC YOU NAPALMED OUT WENT BY.
MAYBE. BUT ORDERS ARE ORDERS, AND STANDING ORDERS ARE TO WAIT. OKAY, GET YOUR CARCASS TO YOUR HOOCH AND GET SOME REST. I GOT A TON OF PAPERWORK NEEDS DOING.
NO WAY! I'M NOT GOING BACK TO A DESK! YOU GET ME BACK TO THE FIELD OR I'M GOING TO THE CAPTAIN! YOU HEAR ME! NO MORE PAPERWORK!
WHO DO YOU THINK YOU ARE!? YOU'LL DO WHAT YOU'RE TOLD AND LIKE IT! YOU'RE LUCKY I DON'T SHIP YOU OUT OF HERE! NOW GET TO YOUR HOOCH!

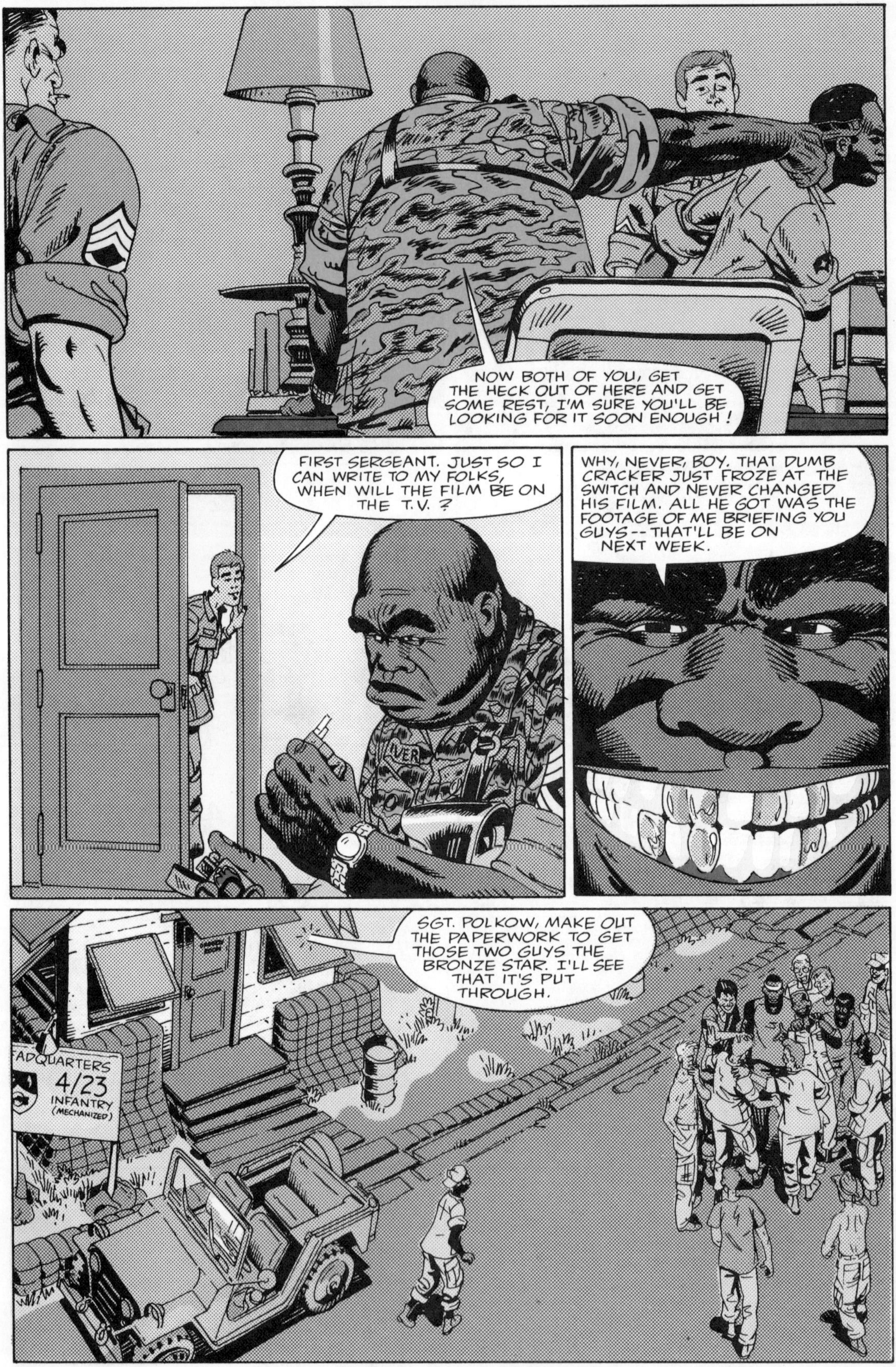
NOW BOTH OF YOU, GET THE HECK OUT OF HERE AND GET SOME REST, I'M SURE YOU'LL BE LOOKING FOR IT SOON ENOUGH !
FIRST SERGEANT. JUST SO I CAN WRITE TO MY FOLKS, WHEN WILL THE FILM BE ON THE T.V. ?
WHY, NEVER, BOY. THAT DUMB CRACKER JUST FROZE AT THE SWITCH AND NEVER CHANGED HIS FILM. ALL HE GOT WAS THE FOOTAGE OF ME BRIEFING YOU GUYS -- THAT'LL BE ON NEXT WEEK.
SGT. POLKOW, MAKE OUT THE PAPERWORK TO GET THOSE TWO GUYS THE BRONZE STAR. I'LL SEE THAT IT'S PUT THROUGH.
EADQUARTERS
4/23
INFANTRY
(MECHANIZED)